Infrastructure Project Finance and Project Bonds in Europe

DOI: 10.1057/9781137524041.0001

Other Palgrave Pivot titles

Annalisa Furia: **The Foreign Aid Regime: Gift-Giving, States and Global Dis/Order**

C. J. T. Talar and Lawrence F. Barmann (editors): **Roman Catholic Modernists Confront the Great War**

Bernard Kelly: **Military Internees, Prisoners of War and the Irish State during the Second World War**

James Raven: **Lost Mansions: Essays on the Destruction of the Country House**

Luigino Bruni: **A Lexicon of Social Well-Being**

Michael Byron: **Submission and Subjection in Leviathan: Good Subjects in the Hobbesian Commonwealth**

Andrew Szanajda: **The Allies and the German Problem, 1941–1949: From Cooperation to Alternative Settlement**

Joseph E. Stiglitz and Refet S. Gürkaynak: **Taming Capital Flows: Capital Account Management in an Era of Globalization**

Steffen Mau: **Inequality, Marketization and the Majority Class: Why Did the European Middle Classes Accept Neo-Liberalism?**

Amelia Lambelet and Raphael Berthele: **Age and Foreign Language Learning in School**

Justin Robertson: **Localizing Global Finance: The Rise of Western-Style Private Equity in China**

Isabel Dulfano: **Indigenous Feminist Narratives: I/We: Wo(men) of an(Other) Way**

Stefan Lund: **School Choice, Ethnic Divisions, and Symbolic Boundaries**

Daniel Wirls: ***The Federalist Papers* and Institutional Power: In American Political Development**

Marcus Morgan and Patrick Baert: **Conflict in the Academy: A Study in the Sociology of Intellectuals**

Robyn Henderson and Karen Noble: **Professional Learning, Induction and Critical Reflection: Building Workforce Capacity in Education**

Graeme Kirkpatrick: **The Formation of Gaming Culture: UK Gaming Magazines, 1981–1995**

Candice C. Carter: **Social Education for Peace: Foundations, Teaching, and Curriculum for Visionary Learning**

Dilip K. Das: **An Enquiry into the Asian Growth Model**

Jan Pakulski and Bruce Tranter: **The Decline of Political Leadership in Australia? Changing Recruitment and Careers of Federal Politicians**

DOI: 10.1057/9781137524041.0001

palgrave▸pivot

Infrastructure Project Finance and Project Bonds in Europe

Emanuele Rossi
Associate Professor of Corporate Finance, University of Milan-Bicocca, Italy

and

Rok Stepic
Project & Commodity Finance Analyst, UniCredit Bank, Austria

palgrave macmillan

DOI: 10.1057/9781137524041.0001

First published 2015 by
PALGRAVE MACMILLAN

Palgrave Macmillan in the UK is an imprint of Macmillan Publishers Limited, registered in England, company number 785998, of Houndmills, Basingstoke, Hampshire RG21 6XS.

Palgrave Macmillan in the US is a division of St Martin's Press LLC, 175 Fifth Avenue, New York, NY 10010.

Palgrave Macmillan is the global academic imprint of the above companies and has companies and representatives throughout the world.

Palgrave® and Macmillan® are registered trademarks in the United States, the United Kingdom, Europe and other countries.

ISBN: 978–1–137–52405–8 EPUB
ISBN: 978–1–137–52404–1 PDF
ISBN: 978–1–137–52403–4 Hardback

A catalogue record for this book is available from the British Library.

A catalog record for this book is available from the Library of Congress.

www.palgrave.com/pivot

DOI: 10.1057/9781137524041

Contents

DOI: 10.1057/9781137524041.0001

DOI: 10.1057/9781137524041.0001

List of Figures

DOI: 10.1057/9781137524041.0002

DOI: 10.1057/9781137524041.0002

List of Tables

DOI: 10.1057/9781137524041.0003

DOI: 10.1057/9781137524041.0003

List of Abbreviations

ADSCR	Annual Debt Service Coverage Ratio
CAGR	Compounded Average Growth Rate
CAPEX	capital expenditures
CEE	Central and Eastern Europe
CFADS	Cash Flow Available for Debt Service
DCM	Debt Capital Market
DSA	Debt Service Annuity
DSCR	Debt Service Coverage Ratio
DSRA	Debt Service Reserve Account
EBITDA	Earnings Before Interest Taxes Depreciation & Amortization
EBRD	European Bank for Reconstruction and Development
ECAs	Export Credit Agencies
EFSI	European Fund for Strategic Investments
EIB	European Investment Bank
EPC	Engineering, Procurement and Construction
FFO	Funds From Operations
IFC	International Finance Corporation
IRR	internal rate of return
IRS	interest rate swap
KPIs	key performance indicators
LCs	letters of credit
LLCR	Loan Life Coverage Ratio
MRA	Maintenance Reserve Account
NPV	net present value
O&M	operations and maintenance
PBCE	Project Bond Credit Enhancement
PBI	Project Bond Initiative

DOI: 10.1057/9781137524041.0004

PEBBLE	Pan European Bank to Bond Loan Equitization
PF	Project Finance
PLCR	Project Life Coverage Ratio
PPP	public-private partnership
SPV	special purpose vehicle
WALL	Weighted Average Loan Life

DOI: 10.1057/9781137524041.0001

Introduction

Abstracts: *Stagnant growth and a decline in infrastructure spending have been major causes of concern in Europe, and different policy measures to address these problems have been taken. The new EU Commission EUR 315 billion Infrastructure Investment Plan for 2015–17 (launched at the end of 2014) and the European Central Bank launch (in January of 2015) of quantitative easing accommodative monetary policy are the latest two initiatives that could have a strong impact on the European infrastructure market. The consequences can be far reaching on the project finance arena. A significant one could be helping to close the market gap existing between the demand and supply of capital at the project bond market level.*

Rossi, Emanuele and Rok Stepic. *Infrastructure Project Finance and Project Bonds in Europe.* Basingstoke: Palgrave Macmillan, 2015.
DOI: 10.1057/9781137524041.0005.

To arrange long-term financing is a crucial task in the initial phase of developing a multi-year capital intensive infrastructure project. Once the specific project case is approved, the next step is to structure the optimal financing available on the banking/capital debt market. One of the main challenges in project finance nowadays, accompanied with the impact of imposed new banking regulations, is how the future funds will be raised to finance capital intensive infrastructure project in Europe, in general, and in regions such as Central and Eastern Europe (CEE), in particular.

This paper combines two topics that attracted our high interest most, infrastructure project finance and its financing structures available in the current market. It is becoming a well-known fact that project sponsors in Europe face more difficulties every time regarding the acquisition of long-term bank financing for infrastructure projects. The described circumstances have caught our interest to a high extent, and therefore, we have decided to analyse the specific market and its alternative project financing options available.

The main objective of the present work is to introduce the best alternative financing solution, which can in the near future act as a substitute for a conventional bank financing, the project bond issuance. We have spotted several recent project finance deals involving project bond funding on European market, and it is adapting quickly to the changing market environment. In addition, with the help of EIB's project bond initiative (PBI) 2020 instrument, project bonds are developing in the right direction and gaining recognition from institutional investors, which is essential for success, since their awareness, in such an early stage, is quite low. Investors firstly need to gain the experience to feel comfort to subsequently purchase project bonds in larger amounts.

However, a few infrastructure project bond financings have already taken place so far, confirming that potential investors from the capital market exist, whose aim is to invest in long-term assets with infrastructure facilities characteristics. Additionally, it is very likely that in the medium-term the involvement of institutional investors would increase competition between lenders, which will further lower the cost of debt. This is extremely well accepted from borrowers, who with project bond solutions, will achieve a more robust and economically more attractive financing structure regarding the fulfilment of the required long-term finance for infrastructure projects.

Moreover, it is paramount to consider the current European economic landscape.

DOI: 10.1057/9781137524041.0005

Anaemic growth, declining investment and insufficient spending on infrastructure have been a major causes of concern in Europe. They have prompted a raft of policy measures to address the problems, culminating in late 2014 new EU Commission EUR 315 billion infrastructure investment plan (best known as Juncker Plan), and in January 2015, the ECB launch of its own long-term Quantitative Easing accommodative monetary policy programme.

These two initiatives better than most describe the current state of the European financial markets and the widespread perception that the source of the investment deficit might be to some extent linked to the financial system. There is a question of whether the problem is a transitory one that is slowly being resolved over time as the effect of the financial crisis fades or a structural one that is going to persist.

For this reason, let us spend a few more words on the significant and far reaching ramifications that these combined efforts could have on the project finance environment. The consequences we envisaged are multiple and in many directions.

The EU Investment Plan for Europe, as we know, aims to revive investment in strategic projects around Europe over the period 2015–17 in order to ensure that money reaches the real economy. This is critical especially for those higher risk long-term projects that are currently finding many obstacles in attracting financial support on the financial markets. The template chosen by EU to promote this initiative seems very much similar to the one implemented with the PBI 2020 Initiative set up in 2012, albeit in a larger and different scale. The planned EUR 315 billion will be mainly guaranteed by mobilizing private investment through the multiplier effect of the new EIB managed and dedicated fund, jointly funded by the EU and EIB, the European Fund for Strategic Investments (EFSI). Initial endowment of EFSI is in fact only EUR 21 billion, 16 billion funded by EU and 5 billion by EIB. The EFSI, once established, should provide risk capital and seed money to catalyse private investment and other relevant public funding. The key to achieving this aim is attracting private investors to stimulate investment and respond to market gaps across a wide range of sectors. The fund is estimated to reach a multiplier effect of 1:15 in real investment in the economy. This is the result of the fund's initial risk bearing capacity and is an estimated average calculated as follows: for every initial one euro of protection by the fund, three euro of financing could be provided to a certain project in the form of subordinated debt. Given that this creates a safety buffer

DOI: 10.1057/9781137524041.0005

in that particular project, private investors can be expected to invest in the senior tranches of that same project. EIB and European Commission experience indicates that one euro of subordinated debt catalyses five euro in total investment: one euro in subordinated debt and on top of that four euro in senior debt. This means that one euro of protection by the fund could generate 15 euro of private investment in the real economy that would not have happened otherwise. Accordingly to EIB evaluation this 1:15 multiplier effect is based on historical experience from EU and EIB programs. This scheme multiplier effect is in our opinion quite similar to that experienced in the implementation of the PBI 2020 Initiative we discuss in Chapter 4 of the present work. EIB Project Bond Credit Enhancement is indeed a cost effective way for the public sector to leverage long-term financing from institutional investors.

The ECB Quantitative Easing can also generate significant effects on the Project Finance landscape. Here it is sufficient to mention a few. The accommodative monetary policy should prolong in the near future a low interest rate market environment in Europe. This provide many immediate consequences on the supply side of capital for the Project Finance market: less attractive yields on government bonds for institutional investors; rock bottom prospective real yields on many low-risk class financial assets around Europe; more appealing yields offered by the low-risk end of the infrastructure assets spectrum; prospective lower correlation between safe asset yields and infrastructure asset promised returns. The latter can improve very much the appeal of infrastructure asset investment as a diversifying tool in institutional investors' portfolios. Besides, for the project bond market, we could have the added effect to stimulate brownfield (operations phase) project long-term bank loan refinancing through relatively lower interest rate bond issuance, with significant funding cost savings for the project sponsors.

In conclusion, the scenario perspectives in Europe for infrastructure project finance activity are quite promising, in particular for the project bond market, and it will be interesting to monitor the future developments.

Moving to the structure and the contents of the present work, we will start in Chapter 1 with a general overview of the project finance (PF) arena and its main characteristics. We will give an in-depth analysis of public-private partnership (PPP) scheme and its advantages/disadvantages in project finance. The PPP structure plays a very important role and in our opinion serves as a key feature for project bonds development

DOI: 10.1057/9781137524041.0005

in Europe. The main differences between greenfield projects (construction phase) and brownfield projects (operations phase) are also considered. This introductory part is needed in order to get acquainted with the variety and complexity of the specialized PF lending world.

The second chapter deals with the European infrastructure project finance market and its recent trends and outlook. The discussion is split between Western Europe countries and the CEE region as the PF-wise degree of maturity and development of these two macro areas is very different. Despite being a relatively newcomer regarding the number of PF deals reaching the financial close, the CEE region has displayed unexpected good performance in terms of PF bank loans default and recovery rates, very much aligned with those reported by more developed regions worldwide.

An added topic, which is gaining recognition, considered in this chapter is the analysis of infrastructure asset as a new asset class for prospective investors. Here, we present how recent developments in European economic landscape tend to strengthen more and more the outlook of those observers that attribute to investment in infrastructure asset the characteristics of a new asset class which can foster the institutional investors demand and interest for own portfolios diversifying purposes.

The following chapter (Chapter 3) will be based on the current banking landscape, examining the advantages and disadvantages comparing a traditional amortizing bank loan versus a project bond funding solution from a general perspective, which will further help us in illuminating the decision-making process for the best available financing structure solution for the prospective project.

As well, we will focus in the following Chapter 4 on the detailed characteristics of the project bond initiative (PBI) instrument developed by the EU jointly with EIB since 2012, looking into their funding experience in transactions coming from Western Europe projects that reached the financial close during the so-called ongoing pilot phase. The basic idea is extracting from the available case histories the main features and the best practices that have triggered the success for financing these projects so far.

The last chapter will be dedicated to case studies in the CEE region. In particular, we have identified the Slovakian market case as the more mature one ready to experiment with project bond issuance, not only for brownfield project or refinancing existing long-term bank loans, but also for the riskier greenfield projects. We will verify if there is enough

DOI: 10.1057/9781137524041.0005

interest from capital/debt market side and if the legislation framework facilitates such transactions. In our case studies analyses we will include, amongst others, two recent motorways infrastructure projects, A11 in Belgium and R1 in Slovakia, from which we will, hereinafter, try to extract the main features, which could be later on applied to the prospective D4 motorway project scheduled to start in Slovakia in 2015/16. We will discuss the reasons why the project bond solution would be the most suitable financing solution for the new D4 project, relying on the prior project bond track record in Europe.

DOI: 10.1057/9781137524041.0005

1
Project Finance

Abstracts: *The project finance topic, even if it is a well-known subject for many practitioners, is still a very complex financing process with many peculiarities not always entirely understood by non-specialists.*

According to Basel II Capital Accord project finance is defined as one of the five subclasses of specialized lending activity. In this sense, it is a very specific lending business with its own rules and procedures. For this reason, banks tend to create within their organization dedicated business units with specialized resources and competences. Hence, there is a need to provide a general overview that can cover not only the main features of project finance but also more detailed aspects such as the public-private partnership (PPP) scheme or the critical differences between Greenfield and Brownfield projects.

Rossi, Emanuele and Rok Stepic. *Infrastructure Project Finance and Project Bonds in Europe.* Basingstoke: Palgrave Macmillan, 2015.
DOI: 10.1057/9781137524041.0006.

1.1 General overview

There are many definitions which can be used to describe project finance (PF). Considering the type of project that will be examined in our work, the definition according to us should highlight PF as a method of raising of funds on a limited recourse basis, with a purpose of developing a capital intensive infrastructure project, where the sponsor is a special purpose vehicle (SPV) entity, and repayment by the borrower will be entirely dependable on internally generated cash flows produced by the project and not necessarily depending on the soundness and credit worthiness of the sponsors.[1] However, the borrower's projects track record plays an important role in the decision-making process.

Clearly, it is arguable to which extent where the borrower is guaranteeing collateral (or other type of contractual remedy) to the lender can be truly called "project finance". However, this is the main reason for shareholders to adopt this kind of financing for infrastructure facility.

Project financing differentiates from corporate financing in a way that PF is a means of financing projects through SPV (legally and economically self-contained legal entity whose only business is the project) as being the borrower for the senior debt. In traditional corporate lending structure, the capacity of raising additional debt depends entirely on the balance sheet strength, looking at the specific company's balance sheets key performance indicators (KPIs). On the other side, project financing enable the shareholders to book debt off-balance sheet, whereby the debt capacity entirely depends on the projected future cash flows. In Table 1.1, we can see other important differences between traditional corporate finance and project finance.

TABLE 1.1 *Corporate financing versus project financing characteristics*

Main characteristics	Corporate financing	Project financing
Guarantees	Certain amount of borrower's existing assets	Project assets; in certain cases additional collaterals required
Impact on financial standing	Reduction of financial flexibility for the borrower	No major effect for a sponsor
Accounting treatment	On balance sheet	Off-balance sheet

Continued

DOI: 10.1057/9781137524041.0006

TABLE 1.1 *Continued*

Main characteristics	Corporate financing	Project financing
Leverage	Depends on borrower's current financial standing	Depends on expected future cash flows generated by the project (leverage is usually much higher)
Adverse Selection	Difficult to differentiate between good and bad borrower and thus assigning the adequate interest rate	Track record and reputation of the borrower difficult to identify since being several shareholders, however the crucial part of assessment is relative to the project performance (expected cash flows)
Moral Hazard	Classical issue, since borrowers do not need to fully engage the money in the investment hold	Cash-flow actively monitored by the lending banks makes hiding money extremely difficult
Information asymmetries	They are present to large extent	Less likely due to the only one project /investment monitoring
Probability of default	Residual value of high importance and looking at the level of intangibles since much value is lost in non-going concern	Mainly dependable on creditors funds and project's assets. Since SPV is set up, borrowers other assets are not point of consideration
Asset substitution	A company might exchange low-risk with high-risk assets to increase the return. On the other hand, the probability of default could be increased for the firm, making debt more difficult and expensive	The risk is relatively very low in PF, where investments are contractually fixed and monitored by the lenders
Strategic bankruptcy	It can be happen when the borrower avoids repaying debt to the lenders closing down the company with a new one which buys important assets	Less probable with verifiable cash flows
Upside potential	Reward and excess return usually belonging just to shareholders. Therefore, issuing of hybrid securities to reach even higher returns since risk/return is unbalanced	It is limited due to financial covenants/ contractual caps

Continued

DOI: 10.1057/9781137524041.0006

TABLE 1.1 *Continued*

Main characteristics	Corporate financing	Project financing
Legal protection of debt holders	Asset based, often with additional collaterals and guarantees	Typically non-recourse transaction. However, very contractual tuned, where debt holders normally negotiate their protection
Valuation/ Financial modelling	Cash flows evaluation is difficult due to hardly predictable parameters. Market comparison makes sense if enough comparable firms available	The valuation has to consider the following conditions: no terminal value (maturity of concession agreement), less volatile cash flows makes it more plausible, market comparison less possible due to the uniqueness of each project

Source: Authors' own adaptation from Gatti (2013).

In other words, we might say that project financing is a complex procedure in which we have an unbiased allocation of risk on a large scale between the various stakeholders of the project. The project itself has a finite life depending on the factors such as length of the concession, contract or licenses. Hence, the PF loan must be fully repaid by the project's life end. In respect to the lenders, they entirely rely on the expected future cash flows projection, which is a mainstream of revenue for the repayment of loan, interest and their fees. Therefore, the project must be "ring-fenced" (legally and economically self-contained) (Yescombe, 2013). The typical stakeholder's structure in a PF deal consists of:

- **Sponsors:** The equity investor of the project company can be a single party or a consortium of sponsors. Their subsidiaries may also act as subcontractors, feedstock providers or off-taker to the project company. In case of public-private partnership (PPP) structure, government may also retain an ownership stake in the project.
- **Government:** The public entity contractually provides a number of undertakings to the project company or lenders, which may include credit support in respect of the procurer's payment obligations under a concession agreement.
- **Contractors:** The performance obligations of the project company to construct and operate the project will usually be done through

DOI: 10.1057/9781137524041.0006

engineering procurement and construction (EPC) contract and operations and maintenance (O&M) contracts.

- **Lenders:** Normally the lending side includes one or more commercial banks and/or international agencies (EBRD, IFC and EIB) and/or export credit agencies and/or bond investors.
- **Advisors:** Due diligence advisors to the lenders which at a minimum will include technical and legal advisors but potentially also financial, insurance, auditing, tax, accounting, market and environmental advisors (depending on the specifics of the project).

The relationships between stakeholders and their roles (services offered) can be observed in the Figure 1.1.

1.2 Main characteristics of project finance

In PF, the project company is a SPV, meaning that the project assets are completely separate entity from shareholders' balance sheets. This fact is providing a few structural advantages to the sponsor including:

- Limited recourse
- High leverage resulting in major impact on the return of the transaction for sponsors (the equity IRR) and additional tax benefits

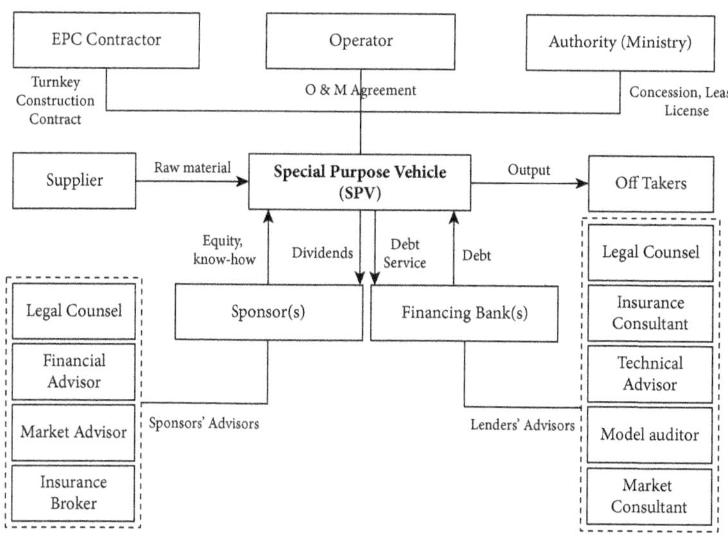

FIGURE 1.1 *Typical project finance structure*

DOI: 10.1057/9781137524041.0006

- Off-balance sheet treatment: only the project's expected internally generated cash flows are essential for the project assessment
- Undertaking hedging strategies to mitigate risks that arise from the transaction

A project financing structure is normally a highly leveraged transaction with a leverage rarely going below 60:40 debt-to-equity ratio, clearly depending on the sector and country risk. Furthermore, high leverage enables lower initial equity contributions, thereby making the project investment a less risky proposition for the shareholders. Additionally, high-level debt financing is bringing advantageous tax shield in terms of deductible interest from profit before tax.

In Figure 1.2, we can observe the five fundamental features representing a PF transaction. As mentioned before, sponsors establish an SPV, meaning no recourse for the creditors on their other owned companies, which is responsible for the project from all different perspectives. For the banks, the relevance of cash-flow is essential when deciding on loan exposure they can afford and approve it to the project company. In every single transaction, external advisors are necessary for the due diligence process to consequently well assess undertaken risks and to allocate them accordingly to the stakeholders.

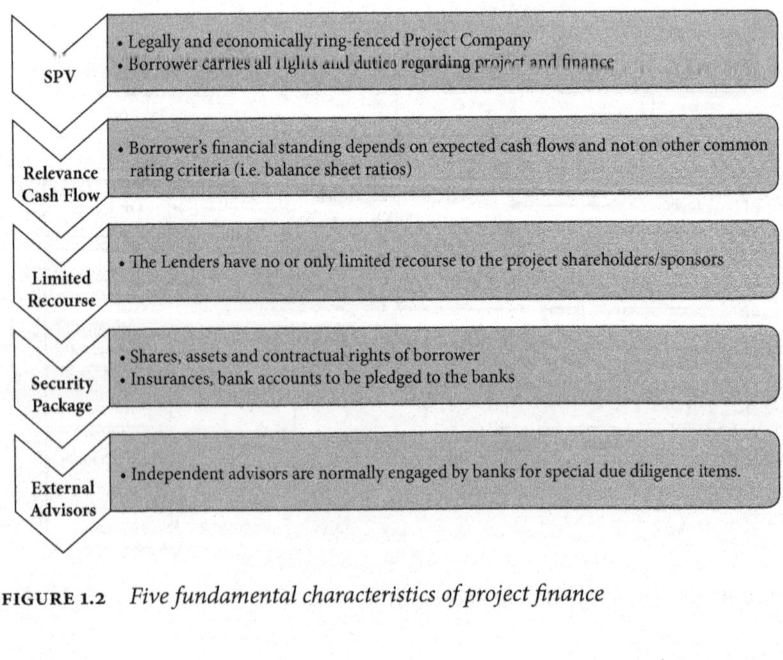

FIGURE 1.2 *Five fundamental characteristics of project finance*

DOI: 10.1057/9781137524041.0006

Adequately addressing risk in PF is a crucial factor since it is responsible for unexpected changes in the ability of the project to repay costs, debt service and dividends to shareholders. Different risks arise from the very beginning stage of the project, starting with construction and continuing in operation period of the project. Particular due diligence process has to be undertaken on the strength and contingent support in respect to the construction contract and other documentation necessary for PF deals. In Appendix A.1, we can observe specific-project risks and their risk mitigants in a typical motorway project example.

1.3 Prerequisites to project finance

There should be meet several precondition requirements in order that project financing is achievable. The project needs to be a sustainable stand-alone entity, for which is forecasted to generate annually enough cash to cover all potential obligation. In addition, the project should be characterized by typical PF constituents. Firstly, construction of the asset during which there are normally no revenues generated. Secondly, there should be involved a type of concession agreement, which gives the right to the project company to build and operate the asset. In the contrary case, a project neither comes to consideration by lending banks and their financial advisory teams. In such case the project could be consider by other lending business units within a bank: Leverage Finance, Corporate Structured Finance and so on. The necessary prerequisites for PF project are the following:

- Sustainable economic performance of the project and bankable financial structure
- Transaction nature should be suitable for project finance
  - Construction period
  - Ramp-up phase
  - SPV (relevance of cash flows)
  - Long-term operating period (e.g. concession arrangement involved)
- Country and political stability
- Stakeholders interest and consequently their involvement
- Sufficient accessible long-term financing
- Identifiable risks and sufficient mitigants (hedging strategy)

DOI: 10.1057/9781137524041.0006

1.4 Public-private partnership

Public-private partnership (PPP) is a specific approach of project stakeholder's structure, where a public service is funded and managed through partnership of government and private sector. Broadly, PPP refers to contractual arrangements, typically medium to long term whereby part of the services that is categorized under the responsibilities of the public sector are provided by the private sector, with clear agreement on shared objectives for delivery of public infrastructure and/ or public services. The PPP can only be present where the long-term concession arrangement takes place for certain social important built structures (motorway, healthcare facilities, prisons and educational facilities). In return, the project company on a monthly or yearly basis receives a predefined revenue stream (so-called available payments) over the concession period from which shareholders of the project company extract returns. PPPs normally do not include service contracts or turnkey construction contracts, which fall in the category of public procurement projects or the privatization of utilities where there is a limited ongoing role for the public sector.

The number of PPP arrangements is on the rise, especially in emerging economies, where governments are constantly encouraging the infrastructure project acting as an essential risk mitigant for the project company. Moreover, an increasing number of countries are including a definition of PPPs in their legislation, each tailoring the definition to their institutional and legal particularities to be as much as efficient. Therefore, there can be recognized many beneficial effects by structuring the project in PPP scheme, which we can see more in detail in the Figure 1.3. Firstly, the project is supplied by private sector know-how and up to date technology, providing better public services through improved operational efficiency also eliminating governmental inefficiencies in infrastructural procurement through tighter contracting and execution. Secondly, the PPP scheme incentivizes the private sector to match projects deadlines and deliver within budgets. Furthermore, PPP transfers the financing responsibility to the private sector, consequently allowing the government to amortize the cost of the asset over the term of the concession (fiscal optimization). Moreover, private sector capacities are developed through joint ownership with large international firms, as well as subcontracting opportunities for local firms in areas such as, electrical works, civil works, security services, facilities management, maintenance services, cleaning services and so on.

DOI: 10.1057/9781137524041.0006

Such structure also enables higher diversification in the economy by increasing competitiveness of the country in terms of its facilitating infrastructure base as well as giving a boost to its GDP and industries linked with infrastructure development (such as equipment, construction, support services and so on). Apart from above described benefits from PPP structure, we can recognize also additional ones:

- Supplementing limited public sector capabilities to meet the growing demand for infrastructure development
- Performance risk: Optimize long-term value for money through appropriate risk distribution to the private sector over the life of the project from construction to operations (maintenance)
- Typically, no traffic neither market risk for the sponsor neither bank, since government as a counterparty within the project agreement accept to bear these risks completely by itself

On the other hand, as any partnership structure, some risks and peculiarities that come along can also be identified. For instance, the development and ongoing costs in PPP projects are likely to be greater than for traditional government procurement projects since there is present an involvement of many more parties and much more bureaucracy work. Considering these facts, there is a requirement of efficiently and transparently structured legal and regulatory framework to achieve a profitable and sustainable solution. We need to be aware that PPP scheme does not really mitigate the total risk that the project entails (limited risk bearing). Hence, private investors (and their lenders) will be cautious about accepting major risks beyond their control, such as foreign exchange rate risk. Subsequently, hedging strategies for such risks increase the price of senior debt facility undertaken. In addition, given the long-term nature of these PF assets and the complexity involved, it is difficult to forecast or envisage all possible contingencies along the project life cycle and problems that could arise and were not described in the documents.

To conclude, PPP transactions are normally distinguished from traditional government procurement arrangements by the fact that they feature fixed-revenues stream to certain level, fixed-term construction contracts and include a requirement to operate the completed facilities pursuant to pre-agreed performance standards over a long-term project agreement. Performance failures can lead to penalties to the operator or in the worst case scenario stop of the payment stream and, ultimately, to the termination of the project agreement. The risk that arises from bad

DOI: 10.1057/9781137524041.0006

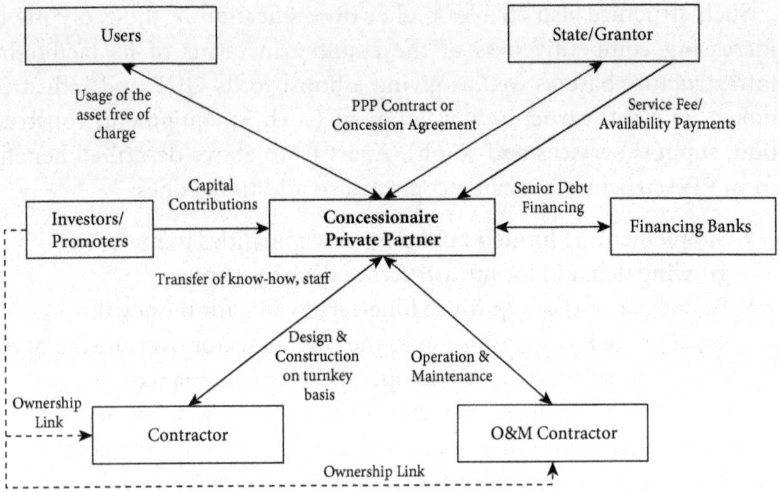

FIGURE 1.3 *PPP structure*

performance of the operator and eventual termination of the concession is usually mitigated by the experience of the contractor. In addition, provisions negotiated and added in the contract documentation, usually permit the government to replace substandard contractors well before termination becomes a possibility. In most of the deals so far, the financial structure of the project company included additional facility of loss-absorbing equity to provide additional credit support.

1.5 Key characteristics of infrastructure project assets

Infrastructure development, no matter if we talk about transport, energy, telecommunications or water, is a crucial global challenge of our times, and its significance is recognized by everyone from the general public. All admit that it is essential for a region's long-term development. Infrastructure characteristics are very particular, allowing generally a highly leveraged transaction on a long-term basis with low volatility of cash flows compared to other investments especially due to generally high participation of government authority in the deals.

DOI: 10.1057/9781137524041.0006

Investments in infrastructure project deals tend to have the following features (EIB, 2012b):

- Government either as a direct client as PPP structure (concession agreement) or through economic regulation.
- Very important services for the general population and businesses, either related to social goods or to physical flows in real economy.
- Long-term nature.
- Generally low level of technological risk.
- Natural monopolies (either due to government policy or to capital intensity/network).
- Very stable cash flows (returns), especially since payments are based on availability rather than demand and payments are typically indexed (linked to inflation).

Due to various economic, political and environmental risks that accompany construction of infrastructure asset, especially in CEE and other emerging markets, many infrastructure projects are facing serious issues when acquiring funds for its financing from financial institutions and from private sponsors. However, PF approach of financing has emerged as a way to mitigate and allocate these risks to the parties that can assess them best and assist in the development and maintenance of the projects.

1.6 Financing the infrastructure projects

Financing a PF deal is a very complex procedure. Part of the financing is backed up from the sponsors in the form of share capital and shareholders subordinated loan. On the other hand, large proportion of debt takes place, in the majority of cases consists of conventional commercial bank loan. Recent surveys suggest that infrastructure is beginning to be viewed as a stand-alone asset and the allocation to this investment class is expected to increase significantly.[2] Commercial banks are still desirable, by borrowers, as long-term debt providers, given their flexibility in renegotiating loans and reacting to new or unforeseen conditions. This flexibility may not be available entirely, for example, from bondholders. However, the global financial crisis has resulted in stricter regulations on banks and their lending requirements, which means that infrastructure

DOI: 10.1057/9781137524041.0006

projects, being funded by traditional long-term loan became limited and other alternative solutions of funding needs to be considered and adopted by project companies. One of the alternative financing structures detected so far and treated as a real competitor to a term loan is a project bond acquired by institutional investors (pension funds, insurance companies, sovereign wealth funds and so on). Deal funding structures usually include the following financing options:

- Sponsor's Equity Contribution (share capital) and Standby equity
- Mezzanine Financing and Subordinated Debt (having the role similar to share capital, with a difference of interest being tax deductible)
- Senior Debt
  - Base facility
  - Working capital facility
  - Standby facility
  - VAT facility
  - Loan remuneration
  - Loan currency
- Bilateral agencies, international financial institutions and multilateral banks, Export Credit Agencies (political risk coverage)
- Alternative financing options:
  - Project leasing (in countries with favorable tax regimes)
  - Project bonds
  - Municipal bonds
- Refinancing loan options:
  - Soft refinancing (waiver-renegotiating conditions)
  - Hard mini perm[3] (change in leverage or the tenor of the loan)
    - Takeover
    - New financing
    - Bond issue at the end of the construction phase
    - Hybrid Solutions-new lending and bond issue

All PF deals have almost indistinguishable fundamental elements mentioned above, which only differentiate in their proportions. However, we may highlight the fact the in the last few years higher than 90 per cent of private sector PF deals were still financed by commercial bank loans. Despite that, since 2013, the project bonds already started to gain increasing recognition with several important project bond issues around the Europe, which can be seen in Table 1.2.

DOI: 10.1057/9781137524041.0006

TABLE 1.2 *Project bond activity in 2013 and 2014*

Issuer/Project	Date	Country	Size (in million)	Coupon	Rating
A7 PPP Motorway	Aug.14	Germany	€430	2.96%	A3
Axione- Digital Infrastructure	Jul-14	France	€189	2.62%	Baa2
Via A11 NV	Mar-14	Belgium	€558	4.49%	A3
Aeroporti di Roma Spa	Dec-13	Italy	€600	3.25%	BBB+
Greater Gabbard OFTO	Nov-13	UK	€305	4.14%	A3
R1 Highway	Nov-13	Slovakia	€1,200	4.78%	BBB+
Birmingham Airport*	Nov-13	UK	£38 £38	Undisclosed	BBB+
Forth Ports*	Nov-13	UK	$160 £60 £35 £80	Undisclosed	BBB
L2 Bypass*	Oct-13	France	€79 €86	Undisclosed	Baa3
Heathrow Funding	Oct-13	UK	€750	4.63%	A–
Zaanstad Prison*	Sep-13	Netherlands	€165 €35	Undisclosed	NR
FHW Dalmore Salford	Sep-13	UK	£72	5.41%	NR

Notes: * Issuers with more than one tranche of bond issuance

Source: Authors' research on bonds' prospectuses.

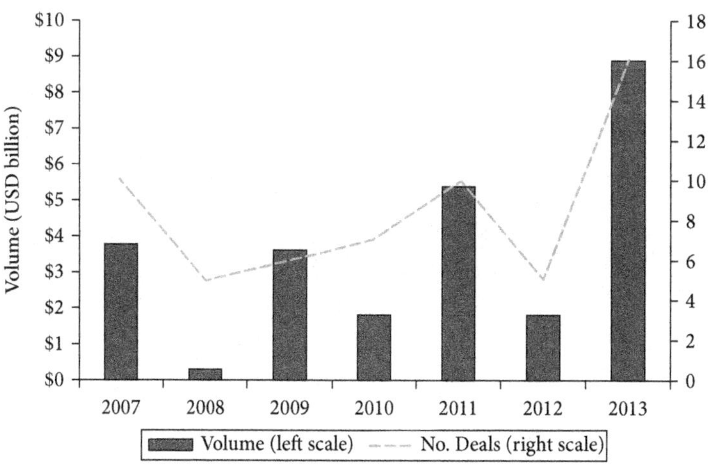

FIGURE 1.4 *European project bonds issuance*

Source: Our research on Dealogic DCM data source

The project bond volume issuance in Europe amounted to USD 8.7 billion in 2013 (the highest yearly volume). This was five times more than in 2012 (USD 1.8 bn) and up 61 per cent on the previous year amount reported in 2011 (USD 5.4 bn) as we can see in Figure 1.4. As an interesting fact, we can add that 16 transactions (20 per cent of the total number of PPP deals) involved institutional investor debt through different financing structures in 2013. Institutional investors provided debt for approximately EUR 2.5 billion to European PPPs at very long maturities (on average 30 years). On the other hand, Figure 1.5 still reminds us the mentioned commercial bank loans lion's share in PF funding on global basis.

1.7 Greenfield versus brownfield projects

In PF, the distinction between greenfield (primary) and brownfield (secondary) project is of high importance. As greenfield are categorized, the projects that still needs to be developed from very beginning and being involved in construction phase first to become operational (operational period) afterwards. On the other hand, brownfield projects categorization indicates the fully operational asset without need of any major

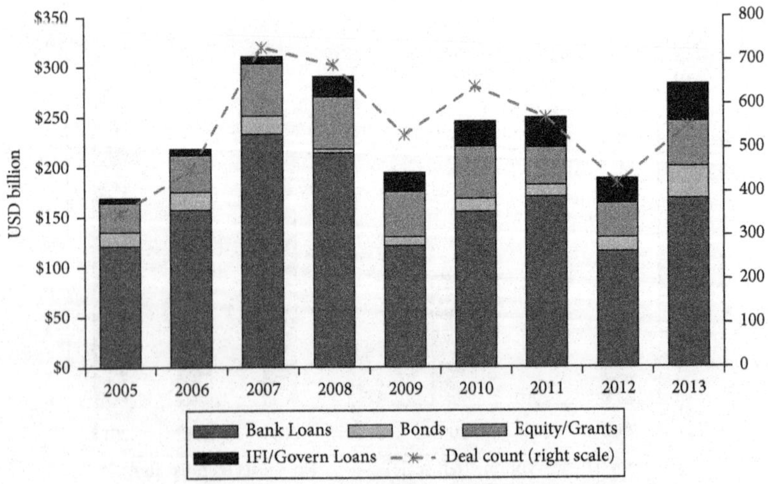

FIGURE 1.5 *Global project finance market by source of funding*
Source: Our research on Infrastructure Journal data

DOI: 10.1057/9781137524041.0006

construction works to be done (except maintenance, reconstruction, expansion). This classification further defines the risks associated with the project's different development phases. In normal circumstances, investors assumes much higher risk for greenfield project since the whole asset needs to be developed: architecture, negotiations with EPC contractors, banks to provide a long-term financing, structuring of legal documentation, due diligence reports and so on. However, surprisingly, there are specific examples that greenfield project's risks level are very alike to brownfield project's ones.

Greenfield projects are generally to be constructed assets for the first time at a specific site. There are different phases in which a project can be running in a certain moment: planning (architecture, different parties selection such as advisors), development, structuring of financing or already in construction phase. The key difference, compared to brownfield projects, is the available asset performing experience, which is zero in case of a greenfield project. Therefore, it is difficult to assess and forecast precisely the asset performance without available historical data. This may lead to a considerably larger uncertainty and risk on the revenue-cost side. The greenfield projects risks are the following:

- Cost side risks (Construction period):
  - Planning
  - Development
  - Receipt of approval
  - Environmental permits
  - Public acceptance
  - Construction (technical risk)
  - Financing availability
  - Negotiation of availability and grace period for financing
- Revenue-side risks (Operational period):
  - Demand uncertainty
  - Price uncertainty
  - New technologies
  - Governmental regulations changes
  - Geographical, political and legal risk

However, in the case of greenfield or brownfield projects, which are involved in PPP scheme, the revenues that are generated in operational period are partly or entirely covered by governmental payments (availability payments) or guarantees; hence, the revenue-side risk is mitigated

DOI: 10.1057/9781137524041.0006

by the project contractual structure. The principal risks that credit providers face arise during the construction period of project and include the following scenarios:

- The project is delayed beyond the envisaged deadline for substantial completion and the project company runs out of liquidity to meet all its obligations before it is entitled to receive the availability payments.
- The project cannot be completed before the long stop date in the project agreement, leading to a potential right of the involved government to terminate the project agreement and pay a termination amount that may not necessarily cover total senior debt, since that calculation will reflect only a cost to complete penalty (including potential additional costs concerning the operating period).
- The EPC contractor (construction company) to which the construction obligations have been passed down needs to be replaced for a variety of reasons specified in the project agreement. For instance, the constructor's inability to perform and deliver the asset compliant with the required standards in the project agreement. On the other hand, there can incur its bankruptcy, insolvency or its inability to complete the project by the constructor's long stop date. It is very likely that such a replacement would entail a higher construction cost. If there are insufficient funds or not envisaged a contingent facility in the structure to cover these additional costs or if the failed constructor cannot be replaced, the project agreement may be terminated and the termination payment may be insufficient to reimburse the total debt facilities.

On the other hand, brownfield projects are already operational and/or the forerunner at the same location can be found. Therefore, such projects have already gone through the greenfield phase, meaning that all the risks arising from the approval processes, development, commissioning, technology, initial demand are in general out of question. This kind of assets are assumed as PF since they are involved in reconstruction, renovation, expansion of the existing facilities or only restructuring of the financing structures due to not performance. The evaluation of such assets is rather simple compared to greenfield assets. The evaluation inputs used can be available historical data (market demand, cash flows, real costs, maintenance needs and so on). However, higher risk of cost blowouts for unforeseen situations might be taken into consideration such as hidden defects, which might be highly important for future operations of the asset. The main risk types arising with brownfield projects are:

- Operational risk
- Regulatory risk
- Market risk
- Geographical, political and legal risk

However, some of greenfield project's risks may return if there is expected extensive reconstruction or expansion of the existing assets.

Further important differences, between greenfield and brownfield projects, can be observed from the investors' point of view. In greenfield projects, investors have to wait some years (construction period), until the asset becomes operational, to receive any return on its initial investment. Even more, in the construction period, which can usually last from approximately 24–48 months, investors are requested to invest large amount of money to build capital intensive facilities and to wait until the assets start to produce certain cash inflows to participate in profit distribution. Investors accept such structure due to very high potential value growth of the asset. However, not all investors are prepared to accept such risks. For instance, institutional investors face many obstacles in respect to undertaking such risks, and therefore, are less likely to participate in a greenfield project. Nevertheless, with certain supportive financial instruments (i.e. PBI 2020) in project financial structure this can become a viable and feasible option and will be elaborated in further chapters of present work.

By contrast, brownfield projects, without hidden defects, will ideally offer stable expected cash flows from the very start in the form of interest payments or dividends. Hence, such project are more suitable for aforementioned risk averse yield driven investors, whereas greenfield projects are more appropriate for growth-style or capital gain investors who are prepared to bear all risk arising in development and construction period.

In conclusion, we need to emphasize that brownfield projects are not necessarily connected with low-risk assets and bond-like returns. To make a good assessment of the asset, we need to review carefully many relevant factors such as condition of the asset, age, maintenance needs,

DOI: 10.1057/9781137524041.0006

current management quality, off-taking agreements contract duration, future economic conditions and so on.

Notes

1 A widely accepted definition of PF is also the one provided by Basel II Capital Accord Framework. According to paragraph 221, "Project Finance is a method of funding in which the lender looks primarily to the revenues generated by a single project, both as source of repayment and as security for the exposure. This type of financing is usually for large, complex and expensive installations that might include, for example, power plants, chemical processing plants, mining, transportation infrastructure, environment, and telecommunications infrastructure. Project finance may take the form of financing of the construction of a new capital installation, or refinancing of an existing installation, with or without improvements".

Basel II classifies PF as one of the five subclasses of specialized lending together with commodities finance, object finance, income-producing real estate and high-volatility commercial real estate (par. 220). See *International Convergence of Capital Measurement and Capital Standards. A Revised Framework* (June 2006) published by the Basel Committee on Banking Supervision at http://bis.org/publ/bcbs128.htm

2 See, for example, R. Bird, H. Liem and S. Thorp (2012), F. Bitsch, A. Buchner and C. Kaserer (2010), Sawant (2010).

3 Hard mini perm is a type of mini perm (short-term) financing that typically require the sponsors to refinance the loan prior to maturity. If not refinanced before maturity, it results in an event of default. Once a project is completed and starts producing income, the sponsor can begin to look for a more long-term financing solution. Hard mini perm financing structure has the ability of the lenders to reprice the loans at then prevailing market rates. Many lenders and borrowers prefer the soft mini perm financing structure that incentivizes, but does not obligate, refinancing of the loans.

DOI: 10.1057/9781137524041.0006

2
European Infrastructure Project Finance Market

Abstracts: *Project finance in Europe has been negatively impacted by recent events; however, there is widespread opinion on the necessity of relaunching a certain level of investment in European infrastructure.*

Even if it is far from clear which are the sources of the investment deficit, infrastructure assets still offer very interesting characteristics to the institutional investors in order to widen their participation in future investments.

Rather than a low demand for long-term capital to be invested in infrastructure projects, there seems to be an insufficient supply of long-term finance. In any case, a higher supply of capital for this particular market segment is not granted and needs to be encouraged and assisted by policy measures.

Rossi, Emanuele and Rok Stepic. *Infrastructure Project Finance and Project Bonds in Europe*. Basingstoke: Palgrave Macmillan, 2015.
DOI: 10.1057/9781137524041.0007.

2.1 Western Europe

In our opinion, it is recommended to divide the European infrastructure PF market into two parts due to the major market characteristics differences. We can also observe significant differences in development and financing structures of project's track record. Thus, we have split the European infrastructure market into Western Europe and CEE. Western Europe consists of the leading Eurozone economies (Germany, France, Italy, Spain and Netherlands), as well as Sweden and the largest non-Eurozone economy in the EU (the UK). Figure 2.1 shows the spending in infrastructure assets by country in 2013. We can see that the three largest economies (Germany, France and UK) account for approximately 65 per cent of total spending in infrastructure, with Germany alone contributing around one quarter of total infrastructure spending in Western Europe. On the other hand, we can already see significant lag behind by the Italian economy, reporting a sharp infrastructure spending/GDP

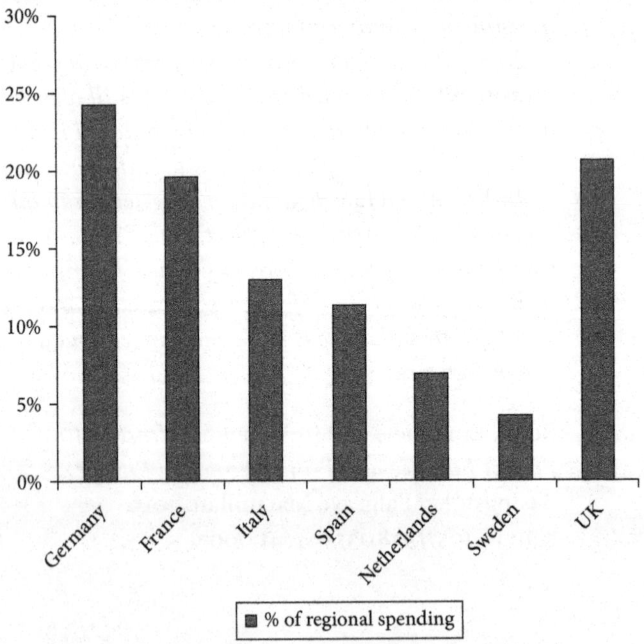

FIGURE 2.1 *Western Europe infrastructure spending in 2013*

Source: Our research on Oxford Economics data source.

DOI: 10.1057/9781137524041.0007

ratio decrease in the last four years. Therefore, infrastructure spending is highly dependable on economy success and consequently public deficit since governments themselves contribute significant funds.

Moving to consider the infrastructure sectors distribution, we can realize that there are big differences in the composition of spending across the economies. For instance, as Figure 2.2 shows, heavy manufacturing remains substantially important in Italy. Furthermore, a large volume of infrastructure spending of Western European countries is delivered in the social and transport sector. The Netherlands invests a greater proportion in transportation infrastructure than any other European economy, with a particular emphasis on seaports and airports, supporting its role as a key trading hub. We confirm that this is very much in line with advanced economies compared to the emerging markets, where the percentage is slightly lower. However, there is quite a substantial difference in the importance of utilities investment though, with Spain leading the pack with close to 40 per cent spending.

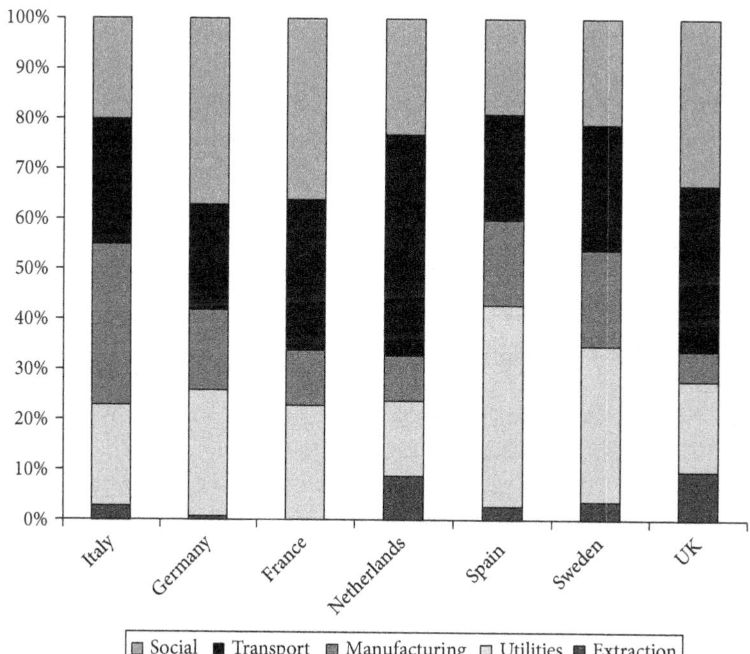

FIGURE 2.2 *Composition of spending across Western European economies in 2013*
Source: Our research on Oxford Economics data source.

DOI: 10.1057/9781137524041.0007

2.1.1 Volumes, developments and financing in Western Europe

As a result of the global lending crisis and the sovereign debt crisis in Europe, global infrastructure markets have been in general decline. Indeed, the European market, which has been historically known as the largest infrastructure project finance market in terms of number and volume of transactions, has been affected to a high extent due to the governmental fiscal tightening and cautious and progressively regulated credit markets. Not surprisingly, most other regions worldwide have also seen a decline in infrastructure investment, although not as steep as across the whole of Europe.

The project bond market, which started to develop in the last decade, was negatively impacted by the financial crisis as pension funds and insurance companies directed their investments into more conservative asset classes. In addition to that, taking into consideration that banks loan tenors have shortened and liquidity requirements being stricter due to Basel III, the infrastructure financing market has a severe need to be supported by public and private (non-bank) institutions.

For instance, in 2013, Europe received approximately EUR 40 billion in project finance investment, and out of this, EUR 33.5 billion was debt, from which we can conclude that until today bank loans have been the main private source for financing infrastructure projects. Total private infrastructure investment in 2012 decreased by EUR 25 billion compared to 2011 and slightly increased to 40 billion during year 2013. On the other hand, the number of infrastructure transactions in Europe dropped to 175 in 2012 from 270 the year before, and in 2013 we can already see slight increase (189), also thanks to EIB's involvement.

The latter move, EIB's project bond initiative, can be classified as an important milestone in European infrastructure policy. It was launched in July 2013 with a EUR 200 million liquidity line for an initial pilot project in Spain. The pilot phase for the initiative, continued through 2013, and full ramp up occurs from 2014 through 2020. As a result, more than just a gradual recovery should happen in Western Europe.

As mentioned before, in the majority of countries, public sector funding in certain infrastructure investments (transport, social) is of high importance; hence, we expect slower growth that in the past as government main focus will be on rebalancing of the public finances. Once again, PPPs are going to play a critical role in the infrastructure transaction

DOI: 10.1057/9781137524041.0007

development, but innovative models and approaches are needed within PPP scheme. This is the best chance for governments to refurbish or to build new infrastructure in partnership with private investors. There is a need for new and innovative financing solutions and setting up capital funds to take equity in projects where there is a clear potential for a positive return on investment.

After the crisis occurrence, funding through financial institutions has become more expensive. At the same time, the proportion of equity, which clearly requires higher returns, in the total transaction value is decreasing what is further increasing the required margin from financial institution due to the level of risk bearing.

Looking at the Preqin Infrastructure Online (2014) data source regarding the investors' preferences, we find some interesting evidence. Seventy-two per cent of Europe-based infrastructure investors favour investments within the region, particularly in West Europe or domestic markets. On the other side, 27 per cent of Europe-based investors will seek opportunities within North America and 46 per cent are open to investments on a global basis. Within the infrastructure asset class, the main access to the market for Europe-based investors is through unlisted fund commitments (82 per cent). This compares to 29 per cent that will consider direct investment opportunities and 14 per cent of investors that seek to invest in listed funds. In addition, Europe-based investors are generally open to investing across all project stages, with brownfield projects (81 per cent) the most favoured, followed by secondary stage assets (75 per cent) and greenfield projects (74 per cent). In addition, in Figure 2.3, we can also observe which type of European-based investors contribute in relative terms to European infrastructure investments. We see that pension funds, private and public, are the biggest contributors, followed by insurance firms and other asset management funds.

Moving to the national level, policies to stimulate infrastructure spending vary from country to country. For instance, UK has a very aggressive infrastructure plan for the future, which consists of 550 projects amounting to GBP 310 billion. However, finding private partners, who would be eager to accept and invest large amount of equity is for now very challenging. Therefore, a new approach to attract investors will need to be undertaken.

In Germany, the PPP concept has recently served as the adequate tool for infrastructure expansion. German infrastructure investments are mainly focused in the incremental upgrading of the country's

DOI: 10.1057/9781137524041.0007

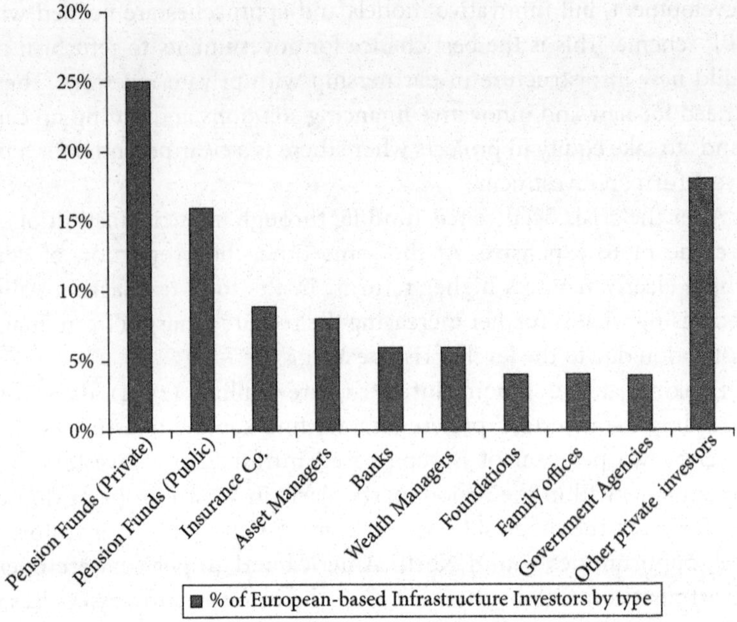

FIGURE 2.3 *Breakdown of European-based infrastructure investors by type*
Source: Our research on Prequin Infrastructure data source.

ageing Autobahn system (for example A7 motorway from Bordesholm to Hamburg/Schleswig-Holstein). In Germany, as in many other Western and North European countries, PPPs are being used to surface the transport and social projects. Furthermore, the changes in the European legislation have resulted in some utilities selling off their regulated activities businesses attracting significant infrastructure investment interest. For example, Germany's decision to close its nuclear plants will trigger significant investment in both renewable energy and the energy grid to support this strategy, increasing demand for capital.

On the other hand, France's current government's preferences are against the PPPs even though the need for infrastructure investments is huge. This is mainly due to the public debt and fiscal policy issue, which do not facilitate PPP project financing. Nevertheless, given France's future investment plans for transport infrastructure, the longer-term likelihood for PPPs in the transport sector appears promising.

Across the Mediterranean region (Portugal, Spain and Italy), the recent crisis has forced many national governments to delay certain

DOI: 10.1057/9781137524041.0007

maintenance and extension infrastructure plans, often reluctantly. In Spain and Portugal, during the economic crisis, many privatizations of public infrastructure assets were happening (airports, public transports), but some of them are now reconsidering since it does not look to be the best option. The Italian government announced plans in early 2014 to raise EUR 12 billion by selling parts in public (state-owned) assets such as postal services, air traffic control systems, shipbuilding, utility transmissions and export credit operations. Italian restraint of privatization policies, which tend to limit disposals to minority stakes in state-owned holdings, faced strong criticism recently, and as a result, the government came up with idea of outselling the stakes of public assets.

In general, we can say that if Western European countries continue to allow their infrastructure to stagnate, they are going to fall behind other most developed regions on the world. This pressure could force more involvement of third party finance creating attractive opportunities for investors. Therefore, opportunities are expected to arise due to the European governmental plans to further encourage private sector investment in infrastructure by addressing the major issues of maintenance and upgrading at a time of severe fiscal constraint at the national and local levels. Besides that, the new European Union's infrastructure plan (Juncker plan) confirms large investments in the sector. The analysis of the European infrastructure investment landscape has shown that it is able to deliver attractive risk adjusted returns over the long term and historical performance can be classified as more stable than many other investible asset classes. However, in order to fully identify all advantages and disadvantages of investing in European infrastructure assets, it is critical to consider a wide range of factors from the social-economic trends to the specific market and investments that drive future performance.

If we look from the perspective of global infrastructure investment made, Western Europe clearly dominates by total deal value as well from the number of deals in the last five-year period. The next two regions, which lag behind and showing very similar levels, are Asia Pacific and North America. More specifically, in 2013, the global project finance market has developed very differently in the various parts of the world. For instance, both, Europe and North America, experienced a decrease in deal count compared to the same period in 2012, mainly driven by the weak financial environment, closing 69 deals for EUR 25 billion and 51 deals amounting to EUR 21 billion, respectively. Other regions around

DOI: 10.1057/9781137524041.0007

the globe experienced an increase in both deal count and deal volume, amounting to 51 deals representing EUR 36 billion in Asia Pacific and 28 deals amounting to EUR 26 billion in Africa and Middle East. Very similar numbers can be observed in the last two years, which is to a big extent thanks to market uncertainty, especially in Europe. However, we strongly believe that with the new infrastructure investment plan launched by EU we can expect significant recovery and an increase in infrastructure investments in Europe.

2.2 CEE

The region has shown a good resilience to the recent financial crisis and is now enjoying rather low economic recovery. Central banks across the region are trying to support growth by lowering lending interest rates or, in countries with relatively high inflation, implementing liquidity support measures. Positives for the region included a clear recovery in other parts of the world, low foreign interest rates and stable or, in some cases, declining commodity prices.

The growth is clearly triggered by the European Union, which is the largest trading partner of CEE. While many emerging markets have been undermined by capital inflows by Federal Reserve's quantitative easing, capital inflow to CEE has been not that significant. In addition, the increasing political and policy risks in the region cannot be ignored when looking into the capital inflows/outflows in the region.

In CEE countries, being EU members, a large portion of infrastructure projects are co-financed by EU funds, whereas countries in the rest of the region are mostly dependent on public budgets and development banks such as EIB, EBRD and ADB, which are playing a vital role in infrastructure financing, especially in countries with low sovereign rating and less developed banking and capital markets. On the other side, pension funds and other institutional investors are scouting these markets for opportunities but have not make a significant impact to date, mostly due to difficulties with the inherent regulatory framework and political risks.

At the moment, the prospects for the infrastructure project deals in CEE are not that clear. Despite the European Commission's efforts to improve the situation, it remains the responsibility of national authorities to create infrastructure programmes and incentives for new investors (institutional, commercial banks, private and so on). There seems to be little clarity, which

DOI: 10.1057/9781137524041.0007

has created uncertainty amongst investors. However, on the infrastructure PF market in CEE, optimism is gaining momentum, expecting that transaction flow will eventually lift up. In Figure 2.4, the main characteristics of today's infrastructure market in CEE are summarized.

2.2.1 Volumes, developments and financing in CEE

The need for infrastructure development in CEE is substantial. Much ground still needs to be made up to raise infrastructure fully to EU standards. In general, infrastructure capital project spending in the CEE region is expected to rise looking into the marked development and substantial infrastructure needs.

Figure 2.5, Figure 2.6 and Figure 2.7 describe the infrastructure market in CEE from different points of view. In Figure 2.5, we can see the breakdown of infrastructure spending by subsector in each country, mostly depending on the needs of country itself. In the major part of CEE region, the countries have sizeable extractive sectors (10–20 per cent of all infrastructure spending), specifically the former Soviet Union countries. On the other hand, the economies in the Central Europe tend to

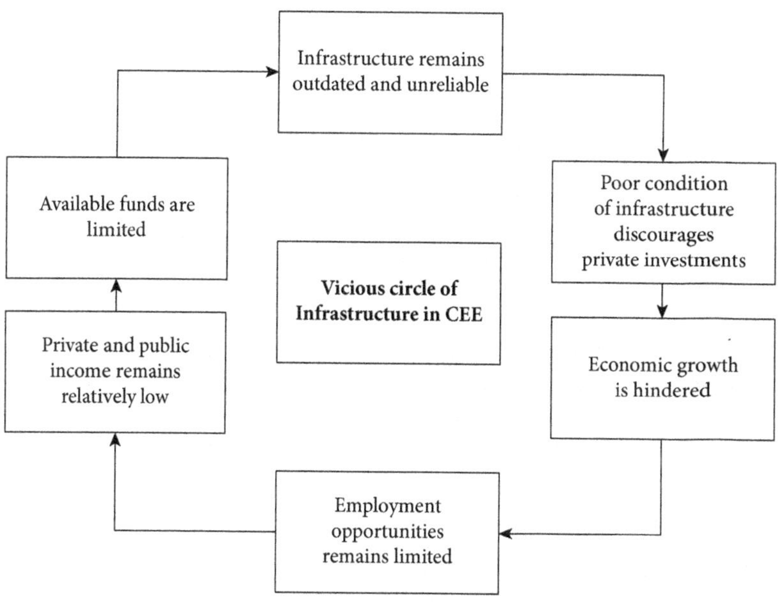

FIGURE 2.4 *CEE infrastructure market characteristics*

DOI: 10.1057/9781137524041.0007

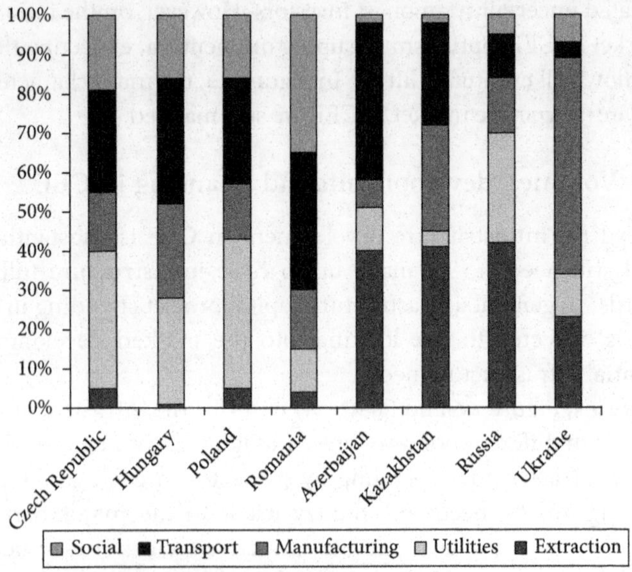

FIGURE 2.5 *CEE infrastructure spending by sector in 2013*
Source: Our research on Oxford Economics data source.

have a much higher degree of investment in transportation spending. This might be, in large extent, due to the availability of EU structural funding. Heavy manufacturing still plays a major role in many of the region's economies, with almost half of all infrastructure spending in Ukraine and a third in Kazakhstan delivered in the chemicals and metals manufacturing subsectors.

In Figure 2.6, we can observe the forecast for infrastructure assets spending in CEE until 2025, meaning that in 2025 it will reach around USD 500 billion (estimated CAGR of six per cent), driven mainly by growth in extraction (Oxford Economics, 2013). If we take a look at Figure 2.7, it is important to mention that currently 59 per cent of investments in infrastructure comes from the Russian Federation, and it is expected to even enlarge its share. However, we cannot overlook the current Russian situation and crisis, which might quickly change the prospective scenario, but over the long term, it is expected that Russia will recover due to outdated infrastructure assets.

What those different sectors have in common is a large need for finance. Given the nature of CEE, structured finance, using term loan

DOI: 10.1057/9781137524041.0007

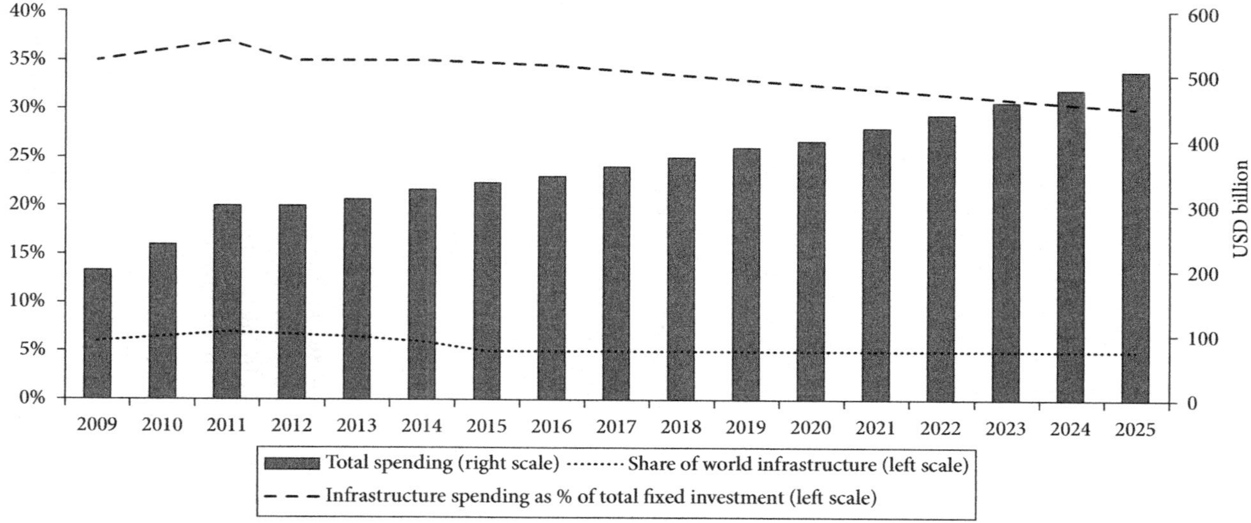

FIGURE 2.6 *Total investment in infrastructure in CEE forecast by 2025*

Source: Our research on Oxford Economics data source.

DOI: 10.1057/9781137524041.0007

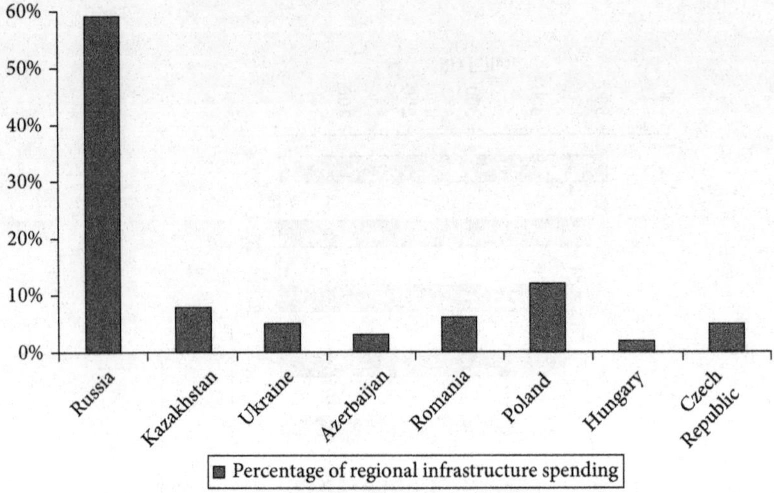

FIGURE 2.7 *Composition of regional CEE infrastructure market in 2013*
Source: Our research on Oxford Economics data source.

financing structures, will continue to play a crucial funding role alongside the quickly developing debt capital markets in the region, especially in the countries with sovereign credit rating of investment grade. Optimal structured finance requires wide and extensive connections with financial institutions as well as demands structuring expertise typically coming from a combination of commitment and longstanding experience.

PPPs have recently been a preferred tool for advancing surface infrastructure (transport) projects. Financing structures have remained broadly similar in recent years: debt (provided primarily by banks) typically makes up to 90 per cent of a project's finance structure and the rest is equity (provided by construction companies, infrastructure funds or other investors). The big change in the post-crisis time is that bank appetite for long-term loans has diminished despite the ongoing demand for it. To fill this particular gap, there has been increasing motivation by banks to involve project bonds and other investors in a long-term infrastructure financing (ING, 2014). For instance, Slovakia undertook a major PPP motorway project, which recently placed bonds privately to investors, including pension funds and insurance funds, with 25 years tenor.

In respect to the equity contribution, historically there has been reluctance from most infrastructure funds to invest outside Poland and Czech Republic, since being perceived as the most mature and stable

DOI: 10.1057/9781137524041.0007

markets in CEE. Most equity investors look for a low-risk profile and are unwilling to accept political and currency risks. However, there was an exception in case of the Budapest Airport project, where Singapore's sovereign wealth fund GIC was involved.

The extended life of infrastructure assets and the long-term nature of the concession agreements with governments make them a suitable match for the long-term liabilities of a pension fund. The accompanying cash flows from the assets are usually stable and predictable due to the usually monopolistic characteristics of the facilities, with high market entry barriers and inelastic demand for use of the assets. Infrastructure investment cash flows such as user tolls, airline charges or rail tickets are often inflation protected by PPP arrangements, and their exposure to default is the lowest compared to other PF assets as can be seen from Figure 2.8. Pension funds may also invest in infrastructure as a diversification strategy as returns tend to have low correlations with returns on other asset classes (OECD, 2013).

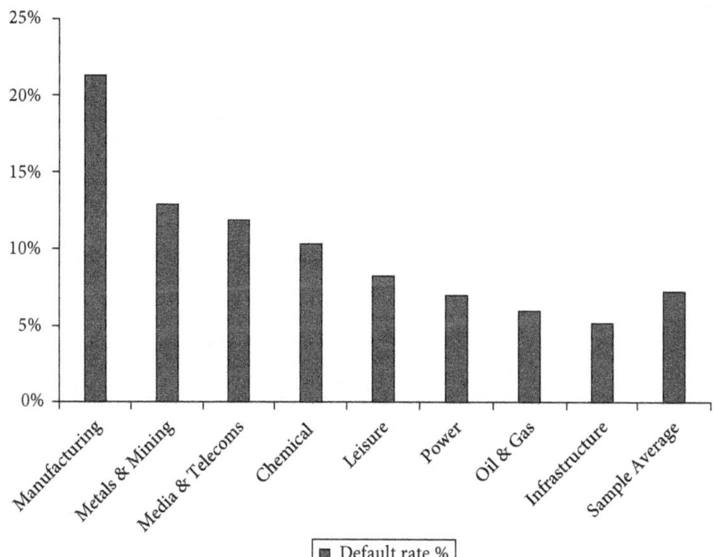

FIGURE 2.8 *Infrastructure PF loan average default rate versus other PF sectors (1983–2013)*

Notes: Infrastructure includes only social and economic assets (roads, rails, ports and airport) Default rates are annual averages across the 1983–2013 period.

Source: Our research on Moody's data source.

DOI: 10.1057/9781137524041.0007

2.3 Infrastructure sectors

Infrastructure is a broad term for different kinds of assets, which has the following definition: it is long-term physical assets that operate in markets with high entry barriers and enable the provision of goods and services. It can be divided in two larger segments: social and economic infrastructure. On the one hand, social infrastructure is a subset of the infrastructure sector and typically includes assets that accommodate social services. For instance, social infrastructure assets include hospitals, educational facilities and prisons. The development and revenues stream of social infrastructure is suitable to PPPs scheme, which have been used successfully to deliver public infrastructure. On the other hand, economic infrastructure supports economic activity and is often demand-based revenue streams (road tolls or landing fees for an airport). In Table 2.1, we describe the infrastructure sectors and specific examples, which should give a better understanding of the sector. Even if there is not always a commonly accepted definition of the perimeter of infrastructure investments amongst many practitioners, we prefer to adopt this much stricter definition based only on social and economic

TABLE 2.1 *Infrastructure sectors and specific examples*

Infrastructure Sector	Examples
Healthcare	Medical facilities Ancillary infrastructure (car parks, training facilities)
Education	Schools (primary and secondary) Tertiary facilities Residential student accommodation
Housing	State or council housing Defence force housing
Utility public facilities	Community and sports facilities Local government facilities Water and wastewater treatment
Transport	Bus stations Airports, ports Availability based roads/traffic risk toll roads Railway
Corrections and Justice facilities	Prisons Court houses

Source: Authors' own research.

DOI: 10.1057/9781137524041.0007

infrastructure investment as we reckon it has the advantage of being much more homogeneous than alternative larger ones, like those that also include power, oil and gas and/or telecom infrastructure assets.

Clearly each subclass of investment within the infrastructure perimeter can generate different expected returns for potential sponsors. Considering the expected target equity IRR across asset subclasses, generally speaking, we can have the following results. The assets involved in a PPP scheme, on average, bring the lowest return (8–10 per cent) compared to other assets since the exposure of equity investor to overall risk is relatively lower. In respect to the IRR level, PPP assets are followed by water, renewables and other regulated utilities' projects, which usually provide a return in the range of 10 to 13 per cent, on average. In the last category of sub-assets, which are bringing on average the highest return (14–15 per cent), are roads, railways, ports, airports. It is logical to expect that these assets normally involve higher levels of risk in respect to the project complexity and construction.

In the following sections, we will discuss in more detail the subsectors that are the core of our stricter infrastructure sector definition: toll roads, airports/ports and healthcare facilities. These subsectors also cover the majority of typical real cases that have reached the financial close in Europe.

2.3.1 Toll roads

Over the last decade, there was an increasing trend of contribution of the private sector to finance roads in both developed and developing economies. However, the current economic crisis has negatively influenced the capacity of many countries to finance such capital intensive projects. Therefore, we may be seeing increased use of the PPP scheme to encourage and promote road construction in the form of more supportive grants as well as minimum revenue guarantees during the operational phase to absorb a certain level of traffic risk, which may arise.

The economics profile of toll road projects depends very much on their function, geography, physical characteristics, contractual structure and traffic profile. The public sector, that is, government, is generally responsible for right acquisition (concession agreement) and political risk and in some cases shares traffic and revenue risk (PPP); the private sector generally bears primary responsibility for remaining project risks (construction, maintenance, safety and so on).

DOI: 10.1057/9781137524041.0007

There are many ways to raise revenues by charging for road usage. However, the principles of taxing road users should meet the economical efficient, equitable, cost little to collect and cannot be evaded. Below, you can see listed several methods:

- Taxes on vehicle fuel
- Vehicle licences
- Vehicle-distance travel charges (i.e. Scandinavian countries)
- Pay-tools (just for specific roads, tunnels and bridges), i.e. Italy
- Vignettes (i.e. Austria, Slovenia)
- Charges on the purchase of new vehicles

The financing available varies, depending on project economics and the country and concession structure, which defines the governmental involvement and support at the end. Funding for private toll roads is primarily in the form of conventional bank loans and sponsor equity. However, in certain examples around the Europe, we can witness the access to capital markets and the involvement of institutional and other investors with bond issuing (Belgium's A11 and Slovakian R1 projects). Large toll road financing in emerging markets and in countries with undeveloped capital markets have relied on foreign capital in majority, whereby funding in countries with highly developed capital markets is normally based on domestic capital as much as possible, looking at the pricing competitive levels.

A very important factor for successfully constructed and managed motorway, which kicks off at very beginning of the project, is the bidding process design for toll road concession, which needs to involve the perfect combination of transparency and competitiveness versus flexibility and private sector innovation. The track record so far confirms that private toll road development is likely to experience modest growth in the near future, meanwhile public resistance to tolling, the time and the cost of implementing concessions will probably limit industry activity. Private toll road development requires that project risks and responsibilities be assigned to the public or private entity that is best able to manage them. As mentioned above, the private sector is better at managing commercial risks and responsibilities, such as those associated with construction, operation and financing. However, in order for a project to obtain financing, public participation may be required in areas such as acquisition of right-of-way, political risk and, in some cases, traffic and revenue risk.

DOI: 10.1057/9781137524041.0007

2.3.2 Airports/ports

This type of infrastructure asset is essential for successful development of the potential catchment area, especially in undeveloped markets. To a great extent, it serves for the further development of the region and attracting population (tourists, investors) or industry (cargo ports). Air or sea connectivity is key to unlocking a country's economic growth potential. The International Civil Aviation Organization (ICAO) defines air connectivity as an indicator of a network's concentration and its ability to move passengers from their origin to their destination seamlessly. Airport investments are centres of thriving retailing activity and are to be assessed as transport infrastructure improvements aimed at addressing a demand for transportation.

The revenue of airport consists of passengers' fees (international and domestic), which is the largest contributor to total revenues. Duty-free service brings a big proportion of revenue as well, clearly depending on the airport location and proportion of international/domestic passengers' ratio. Other food and beverages and fuel services can add a significant revenue proportion as well. According to recent developments, airports are now focusing on increasing non-aviation revenue as a way to cope with the volatility of the airlines business cycle, including selling to non-flying passengers, which is a big change from pre-2000 when only a third of airports were trying to tap the wallets of those customers.

The main risk arising at the airport are traffic volumes (market risk), which cannot be guaranteed and mainly depends on the airlines strategies and catchment areas development and attraction. Before making a decision to build a new airport/port, the research should be conducted, reviewing the competitive facilities in surroundings, expected traffic volumes, environmental and social issues with the construction site and so on.

Typically government involvement is not at very high levels except from a regulation point of view. Government's responsibility is to organize a bidding process at which the airport operator with the highest offer (bid) for operational rights receives a concession for approximately 30 years to manage the airport and its maintenance. With the concession assigned, also comes annual leasing payments, which are derived from the bid amount offered at the bidding processes. It needs to be emphasized that leasing payments represent a large proportion of operational costs for the airport operator.

DOI: 10.1057/9781137524041.0007

But as the industry shifts from survival to expansion mode, new issues are emerging: the risk of over-expansion in airline capacity, the difficulties of expanding airport infrastructure and airspace capacity where it is most needed and the long-term environmental challenges of a rapidly expanding global aviation industry.

2.3.3 Healthcare facilities

Many countries are undergoing major healthcare infrastructure developments in response to growing and ageing populations in addition to greater expectations of health services from a community due to the technology and science progress. Moreover, healthcare facilities are normally quite risky investments. Recently, the most widely structure used is the PPP scheme, and PF techniques are increasingly recognized as a useful and appropriate tool. The PPP structure is extending to emerging markets as well, where the risk of unstructured PPP legislation and corruption represents major risks in such markets. However, the recently closed transaction of Mersin Healthcare Campus (shortly two other hospitals) in Turkey is proving the contrary and shows progress in respect to that.

Risk identification, transfer, sharing and operating management are key factors of the whole structure in order to successfully assess the overall risk and fairly evaluate the expected return. While the government or Ministry of Health typically bear the market risk (demand for health services), other key risks, such as those related to construction and management of commercial activities, are typically assigned to the parties that know best how to recognize and mitigate such risk, often represented by private entities. A corporate finance perspective is fundamental for developing a proper business model, where financial cash flows are projected along the life cycle of the investment. Capital structure issues, focusing on optimal leverage, must be deeply analyzed. The design and operation management of healthcare campuses makes an important impact on the quality of delivery of healthcare. More and more innovative design supports patient pathways and enables staff to work effectively, making a significant contribution to both patient outcomes and the efficiency of the staff and facilities.

Within the healthcare sector, revenues and demand for services mainly depend on the public and are clearly predominant. There are also other revenues for the private investor, which are represented by commercial

DOI: 10.1057/9781137524041.0007

activities related to the core investment (i.e. parking, restaurants, shops within the health campus and so on). The larger the commercial part, the higher the levels of demand risk that the responsible private investors bear.

The price to be paid from the government to the private concessionaire depends on the operational cost of the healthcare project (capacity) and is divided into three synergistic components:

- Construction costs contribution, to be paid according to the building costs and phases
- Periodic availability payments for making the facilities working and available during the operational period
- Economic margins on commercial services contracted out to the private party

Investment risks associated with healthcare assets mainly concern:

- Risks linked to the construction site (highly technological equipment)
- Risks of planning, developing, engineering and construction (very complex facilities)
- Procedural, contractual and legislative risks (normally PPP legislations and contracts require time-consuming negotiations between authority, sponsor and commercial banks)
- Financial risks (capital intensive assets, exchange rate and interest rates)
- Governance and sponsor risk (question of experience)
- Operating and performance risks
- Market risks

2.4 Infrastructure: a new asset class?

Infrastructure investment attracts more consideration from institutional investors, and considering their aims, we can ask if infrastructure can be seen as a new asset class for their investment portfolios. Many researchers and practitioners are looking in that direction (Weber and Welfen, 2010). The government bonds' and other similar low-risk investment instruments' returns are reaching rock-bottom levels in Europe. And the current European market situation, which is to large

DOI: 10.1057/9781137524041.0007

extent influenced by accommodative monetary policy, culminating in ECB Quantitative Easing launched in January 2015, should maintain such low levels of financial returns for the foreseeable future. Moreover, even some deflation risks are present as well, which can be an added obstacle to convince market participants to commit investment and to increase their debt burden. The above described market situation and the fact that pension funds and insurance companies' portfolios consist mainly of such low-risk assets make them extremely uneasy and eager to find new investment opportunities, which will assure them higher real returns while keeping the overall portfolio at relatively low level of riskiness.

Looking at the European financial market landscape, we can see that the particular characteristics of infrastructure assets match to a great extent the institutional investors' highly regulated requirements. First of all, the ability to match long-date assets-liabilities and bring "real" return are very important aspects. Second, the assets usually operate in an environment of limited competition, inelastic consumer demand for asset use and capital intensive industry creating barriers to entry; therefore, we can see them often as natural monopolies (concession, regulation). Third, a very low correlation to other asset classes, stock and bond assets exists, enabling institutional investors to diversify the portfolios more and reach lower overall portfolio risk. In this direction, ECB accommodative monetary policy can foster the decoupling between safe financial assets and infrastructure asset returns dynamics. Furthermore, most of the asset performance, in an equity investment case, derives from dividends with a modest expectation of capital appreciation and a very stable cash inflow. There also exists a possibility of superior returns to early investors, which is proportional to higher risk bearing (in the construction phase). However, if there is an involvement of EIB PBCE instrument (see Chapter 4), this risk is to great extent mitigated and returns remain at relatively high levels for a given class of risk.

On the other hand, yields for debt infrastructure investments are much higher than those on governmental bonds and similarly rated corporate bonds under comparatively low default rates and high recovery rates. Based on primary rating agency data source (Moody's, 2015), the average long-term historical default rate (computed according to a standard Basel II definition of default[1]) for infrastructure PF industry is confirmed to be quite low at a 5.2 per cent level, and it is substantially

DOI: 10.1057/9781137524041.0007

below the average default rate of 7.2 per cent for the more comparable industries in the unrated PF bank loans universe.[2] This evidence suggests that default risk for infrastructure projects is rather low, especially where project revenues are based on availability based payment mechanisms as opposed to being exposed to market demand risk. In the PPP segment, the default rate is as low as 4.4 per cent, supporting the view held by many market participants that PPP can be seen as a discrete subsector lying at the low-risk end of project finance spectrum. Overall, we could confirm that such characteristics match very well with the institutional investor needs.[3]

In Table 2.2, we summarize the details on default performance of bank PF loans to specific industries. Here, the PF infrastructure industry is defined in the more limited scope including only social and economic/transport (road, rail, ports and airports) infrastructure investment. It is very clear that average default rates vary significantly by industry. For example, PF bank loans default rates for infrastructure and oil and gas are substantially lower than default rates for manufacturing, metal and mining, and media and telecom. Moreover, if we move to consider a selection of relevant regions worldwide, we can observe in Table 2.3 that the default rate is at very low level in Eastern Europe and Western Europe, with 4.8 per cent and 5.2 per cent, respectively. The highest default rates findings in other areas, such as South East Asia and Latin America regions, gives us a strong argument in support to the relatively low-risk European infrastructure PF habitat.

TABLE 2.2 *PF bank loan default rates by selected industry*

Industry	Average Default Rate** %
Infrastructure*	5.2%
Manufacturing	21.4%
Media & Telecom	12.0%
Oil & Gas	6.1%
Power	7.0%
Metals & Mining	13.0%
Average (simple)	10.8%
Average (weighted)	7.2%

Notes: * Infrastructure includes social and economic assets (roads, ports and airports)
** Default rates are computed annually according Basel II definition of default across 1983–2013 period

Source: Our research on Moody's data source.

DOI: 10.1057/9781137524041.0007

TABLE 2.3 *PF bank loan default rates by selected region*

Region	Average Default Rate* %
Eastern Europe	4.8%
Latin America	14.8%
North America	9.9%
South East Asia	10.0%
Western Europe	5.2%
Average (simple)	8.9%
Average (weighted)	7.2%

Notes: * Default rates are computed annually according Basel II definition of default across 1983–2013 period

Source: Our research on Moody's data source.

Table 2.4 provides main evidence regarding the recovery rates[4] reported in case of default, with statistics split by comparable industry and by a selection of macro regions for the same PF bank loans sample.[5] Here, we can observe that in the infrastructure sector, the recovery rates are, on average, amongst the best (higher), meaning a relatively better performance in terms of minimizing loan economic losses during work out procedures (see Panel A); however, from a regional perspective, we do not notice large differences across regions (Panel B). The data shows a broad consistency of recovery rates across regions lying in the range of 71.8 per cent to 82.2 per cent.[6] The distribution of recoveries by project phase confirms instead that a higher risk is embedded in the greenfield/ construction type of PF loan versus brownfield project loans with a 69 and 82 per cent average recovery rates, respectively. In general, recovery performance, as expected, is much better for projects that default later in the project life cycle.

Looking through the same Moody's database, we can also highlight that recovery rates for PF bank loans and for corporate bank loans are very similar, despite higher leverage and long tenor, which are typical for project finance loans, are generally associated with higher risk loans. This clearly shows that PF debt perform very well, limiting loan economic loss in post default phase. An added critical aspect to mention is that recovery rates for PF defaulted assets are substantially uncorrelated with default rates. The recovery rates for PF loans emerging from default were in the range of 60 and 88 per cent showing high independence from the economic cycle, contrary to generally expected evidence. For

TABLE 2.4 *PF bank loan recovery rates by industry and by region*

Panel A Recovery rates by industry

Industry	Average Recovery Rate** %
Infrastructure*	72.6%
Manufacturing	49.2%
Media& Telecom	60.2%
Oil & Gas	73.4%
Power	88.5%
Metals & Mining	58.3%
Average (simple)	67.0%
Average (weighted)	76.4%

Panel B Recovery rates by region

Region	Average Recovery Rate** %
Eastern Europe	78.2%
Latin America	80.2%
North America	71.8%
South East Asia	82.2%
Western Europe	73.8%
Average (simple)	77.2%
Average (weighted)	76.4%

Notes: * Infrastructure includes social and economic assets (roads, ports and airports)
** Recovery rates are annual averages across 1983–2008 period

Source: Our research on Moody's data source.

conventional corporate bank loans, in fact, we normally find a significant negative correlation between recovery rates and default rates, as when default rates rise due to a negative economic cycle the recovery performance tends to worsen. PF infrastructure assets are substantially less correlated with a number of factors which impact general corporate debt/asset performances.

All this evidence supports the idea that even if project finance infrastructure assets are highly leveraged, thinly capitalized special purpose vehicles with low financial flexibility, PF debt contracts are still structured to be resilient to a wide range of potentially severe risks, minimizing in this way any post default loan economic loss. In this sense, risk allocation, structural features, incentive structures, which are peculiar to PF infrastructure asset class, have proved in real market test to be quite effective.[7]

Returning to our initial question whether infrastructure assets could be considered as a new asset class, the answer cannot be completely positive, despite the promising evidence discussed so far. Still, we have a few obstacles that are holding back infrastructure investments as a full emerging asset class. The following aspects must be considered.

From an institutional investors potential demand perspective, we can highlight the typical European large pension funds asset allocation in Figure 2.9, which shows us that infrastructure investments amount to only around one per cent of the overall portfolio, and there is evidently large space available for growth of equity/debt infrastructure assets in a typical long-term institutional investor portfolio.

This encouraging starting situation is largely offset by several aspects needed to change to infrastructure assets in order to become a significant part of institutional investors' portfolios. In particular, critical mass and benchmarks will be required for a true asset class. Investors need to become more familiar with such assets, and they want to observe a certain historical track record, since at the moment, it is still a new market with a lack, for example, of bond market underwriting so far. We believe that the first wave of infrastructure assets which perfectly match the investors' requirements are assets involved in PPP scheme (stable cash flows,

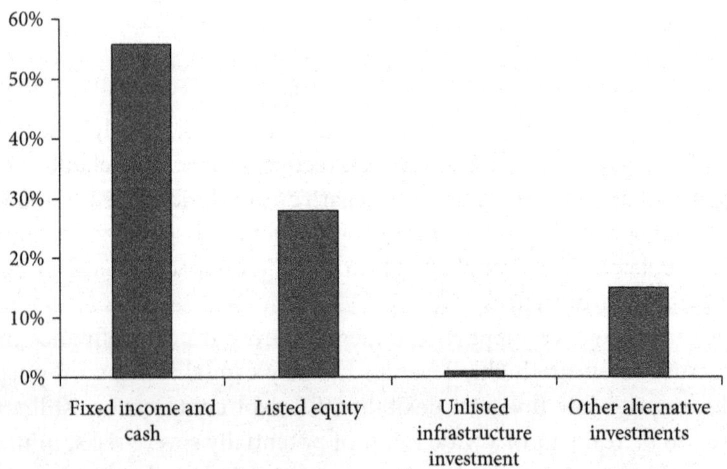

FIGURE 2.9 *Average asset allocation of a typical pension fund*

Source: Our research on OECD data source.

DOI: 10.1057/9781137524041.0007

lower demand risk, higher regulation), and only after these assets have become common practice in institutional investors' portfolios, investors will widen their spectrum of possible asset allocation (ports, airports).

Despite this, the lack of available, reliable and well recognized benchmarks for the asset class is certainly the most critical aspect. The availability of those benchmarks is paramount to guarantee the full emergence of the new asset class in the investors' perspectives. Substantial investment in infrastructure by long-term investors cannot take place without adequate measure of expected performance and risk that only benchmark indices for long-term infrastructure investments can provide. Those benchmarks can inform asset allocation decisions by market participants as they need to know what risk and performance to expect over time and in different economic environments. The availability of those benchmarks could also help regulators in order to adapt ever evolving regulatory frameworks. For example, regulators in Solvency II framework clearly require empirical evidence before they can consider adapting the risk-weights that are currently applicable to long-term investment in infrastructure in the insurance industry. The lack of this kind of evidence results inevitably in higher capital charges/allowances for long-term infrastructure investments discouraging institutional investors in taking on substantial positions.

Building a new class of benchmark of this type is a very complex task for a number of reasons: the illiquid and less frequently traded characteristics of the infrastructure assets; the very long cycle (20–30 years normally) of projects that impedes collecting complete information for the majority of ongoing projects; the difficulty of assembling a comprehensive database on a globally dispersed infrastructure projects with the degree of granularity needed for this type of exercise; and, last but not the least, the need to select a widespread accepted standard definition of the perimeter of infrastructure investment. Many of these aspects have been addressed by a few ongoing recent researches. Blanc-Brude (2014), for example, is proposing a roadmap in order to promote and develop a new class of unlisted infrastructure investment benchmarks,[8] both equity and debt ones, which is very interesting. Much work still needs to be done in this direction as we are only at the beginnings.

In conclusion, it is clear that infrastructure investment experience by the institutional market will take time, and the progress may be tiered.

DOI: 10.1057/9781137524041.0007

Notes

1 According to Basel II Framework, a default is considered to have occurred with regard to a particular obligor when either or both of the two following events have taken place.

a) The bank considers that the obligor is unlikely to pay its credit obligations to the banking group in full, without recourse by the bank to actions such as realizing security.

b) The obligor is past due more than 90 days on any material credit obligation to the banking group.

See *International Convergence of Capital Measurement and Capital Standards. A Revised Framework* (June 2006).

2 The data on average default rates are computed considering a sample of 5,308 projects originally financed with an unrated PF bank loan across a period starting from 1983 until 2013, Moody's (2015), *Default and Recovery Rates for Project Finance Bank Loans*. The default rate is computed as the ratio between the number of defaulted loans and the total number of existing PF loans. The total PF debt raised in PF bank loan sample during the period investigated has been up to USD 2,623 billion.

3 Moreover, PF bank loans exhibit significant improvement over time in the marginal annual default rate performances as time passes from the origination date. In particular, PF bank loans trend toward marginal default rates consistent with a single-A category rating by year ten from financial closing. This seasoning feature is unique for PF loans and differentiates the behaviour of project finance bank loans from typical corporate bank loans (Moody's, 2015). This behaviour can clearly be explained by the fact that in the project finance case the default events tend to be clustered in the first three to four years from financial closing. When the project becomes up and running, the default risk declines very quickly, normally after four years from origination.

4 Recovery rate is the percentage of the nominal principal amount of the defaulted loan that has been realized following that loan's emergence from default. Emergence from default is deemed to occur in any of the events set out below:

- repayment of overdue interest;
- restructuring with no consequent default;
- liquidation.

5 In this case, the period under investigation for the recovery rates computation is limited to 1983–2008 (Moody's, 2010).

6 In Panel B of Table 2.4, a few regions, like Africa, Oceania and so on, have been excluded as the Moody's database sample sizes were too small to support statistically robust conclusions.

DOI: 10.1057/9781137524041.0007

7 An added evidence drawn on a separate Moody's analysis shows that ratings on project finance debt have historically provided roughly the same level of accuracy as corporate ratings in differentiating defaulters from non-defaulters (Moody's, 2009).

8 F. Blanc-Brude (2014) also advocates the necessity of establishing a common reporting standard to be adopted by PF sponsors in order to facilitate relevant information availability helping to assemble those specialized sector benchmarks.

DOI: 10.1057/9781137524041.0007

3

Bank Conventional Lending versus Project Bond Solution

Abstracts: *Project bonds, which can act as a substitute for a conventional term loan bank financing, are surely the best alternative financing solution. We have noticed several recent project finance deals involving project bond funding in the European market, and it is adapting quickly to the changing market situation. From a general perspective, it is important to highlight and examine the advantages and disadvantages comparing a traditional amortizing bank loan versus a project bond funding solution. This is crucial in order to help us illuminate the decision-making process for the best available financing structure solution for prospective projects.*

Rossi, Emanuele and Rok Stepic. *Infrastructure Project Finance and Project Bonds in Europe.* Basingstoke: Palgrave Macmillan, 2015.
DOI: 10.1057/9781137524041.0008.

 DOI: 10.1057/9781137524041.0008

3.1 Banking landscape

The regulatory landscape for debt will evolve further with the implementation of Basel III requirements, which are slowly but surely stepping into the international bank regulation framework. Mentioned pressures on banks' balance sheets have constrained bank long-term lending, and as such, they are no longer best positioned for long-term PF lending. Thus, there have been many talks about non-conventional bank funding options for infrastructure deals in the future. The banking landscape should change, since major players scale back in some areas and invest in others in response to changing liquidity and capital requirements. The current lack of liquidity in the banking market combined with rising bank funding costs are causing major changes in the infrastructure project funding. It is widely expected that the global banking sector may have to increase the price and face difficulties raising the amount of long-term funds (term-loan facility). As seen, banks and governments, driven by deficit reduction and new regulations, are likely to continue holding back in terms of infrastructure investments. However, institutional investors and the financial markets that recycle their capital have the potential possibilities to step into the funding gap. They offer a huge and growing pool of savings that could be rationally and profitably invested in the infrastructure sector.

In the absence of long-term lending, a less than significant number of European PF deals have been structured with bond issuing, especially due to institutional investors being cautious to invest in the low BBB investment grade range, partly the reason stand behind their regulatory requirements (e.g. Solvency II). In order to successfully raise enough investment funds for future infrastructure projects, sponsor and financial advisers will need to find the optimum balance between public and private money supply. According to many observers, banks will continue to sell their large infrastructure debt portfolios to other financial institutions to reduce the amount of risk-weighted assets (RWA). However, many market players will try to create multi-investor institutional debt funds or find structured products that can mitigate the risk of senior debt. The debt capital markets will need to provide funds for infrastructure financing because it is not reasonable to think that bank debt will meet all current and future demand.

DOI: 10.1057/9781137524041.0008

In the aftermath of the credit crisis until 2013, the market for project bonds in Europe was non-existent. The challenge that project bond market currently faces is to ensure that the market will be sufficiently well organized by the time that governmental budget for infrastructure project dries out. This will clearly involve bond investors bearing more project risk in return for the same risk adjusted returns. Additionally, rock-bottom interest rates on government bonds have left insurers and pension funds eager to find higher-yielding long-term investments that they can use to meet obligations to policyholders payable decades in the future.

It is well known that pension funds, insurance companies and other institutional investors are seeking to diversify their current investment portfolio and asset allocation with yields higher than government bonds, delivering stable, long-term income that perfectly matches their liabilities and fills the gap left by defaulted securitization products. Nevertheless, institutional investors focus is still mainly the bonds with "A" credit rating, which has the right risk/return combination in respect to the financial regulators. Hence, the only acceptable rating class rarely covers greenfield projects, because of the risks of construction delays and cost overruns, especially without any supporting instruments in construction such as PBCE (see Chapter 4).

While there is a general consensus that capital markets might be in a very favourable position at the moment to become one of the very important funders of PF deals, it is not happening yet. It will require a different political leadership approach, innovative thinking by financiers, and new economic incentives to persuade different investors into the peculiar world of infrastructure. The main obstacles for the development are the following (EIB, 2010):

- Commercial banks still assume debt capital market as a competitor. PF has been traditionally a banks' preserve and a major source of fee business for them. They are interested in capital markets mostly to the extent that it enables them to refinance their existing long-term commitments and roll over their portfolios. Consequently, banks' RWA disappear.
- Borrowers are generally more comfortable with banks (over which they can exert a much stronger commercial control) and fear the "uncertainties" associated with capital markets (lack of early commitments, inflexibility of a "market" dictating its conditions).

DOI: 10.1057/9781137524041.0008

- Investment bankers and advisers, in some cases, may be keen to develop this business but will only invest the considerable upfront costs necessary to arrange complex project bond issue if they see a perspective of repeating the deal structure.

In addition, other factors have been recognized which can slow down the project bond progress (Yescombe, 2013):

- A concern that investors would not take construction risk
- Negative carry[1]
- Implementing effective decision-making procedures for bondholder
- Project procurement models that favoured the pricing certainty offered by lending banks
- Project bond's credit risk profile and performance monitoring are very complex tasks and consequently very costly
- Credit rating grade at the bottom end of investment grade
- Bonds insurance difficult to obtain for infrastructure transactions

Lately, we can observe an increased move toward shorter-term loans structures under which the borrower is incentivized to refinance after several years throughout the use of cash sweep mechanisms[2] and increases in margins. Banks will persuade sponsors to accept the refinancing risk by structuring loans in shorter tenors. Tenor can be expected to be a key negotiating point for the time being.

Many of traditional project finance bank lending have been impacted by imposed capital adequacy requirements in a way that they became no longer active in respect to the infrastructure financing and they refocused on their "core banking" segment. Since the liquidity gap needs to be filled, there are a significant number of potential investors out there looking to gain access to the best assets in the infrastructure transactions market, which will lead to a high level of competition and eventually pressures on bond pricing. However, there are clearly many banks with liquidity issues. Nevertheless, there is still sufficient capital for the highly profitable and sustainable deals, with the reputable sponsors, with the right financial structures and with the acceptable country risk. Although, the perseverance of the banking market has been highlighted, it may see a very different future, involving a much bigger investor base mix, combined with structures that involve both short-term and longer-term pieces for these different investors.

DOI: 10.1057/9781137524041.0008

3.2 Key characteristics of bond financing

The market for project bonds for infrastructure transactions is only in its infancy. However, the EIB took an incentive to strengthen the awareness that project bonds can fundamentally play a more important role in financing the infrastructure project market. It might contribute a great part to the development and revitalizing of the capital market for infrastructure financing. Due to the current market situation, it can be expected that project bonds will become an increasingly important funding instrument in Europe over the medium term.

In Figure 3.1, we sum up the most important facts that triggered the development of project bonds in Europe. There are four categories that bring a significant impact to the evolvement. First of all, there are clients looking for more competitive pricing to finance the projects. Secondly, institutional investors constantly seek to diversify their portfolios. Thirdly, regulatory framework limits the conventional bank lending the funds, making them unavailable to serve all of the infrastructure project demands around the Europe. Ultimately, several supportive instruments for project bond funding such as PBI, PEBBLE, Hadrian's Wall and so on[3] have emerged on the market.

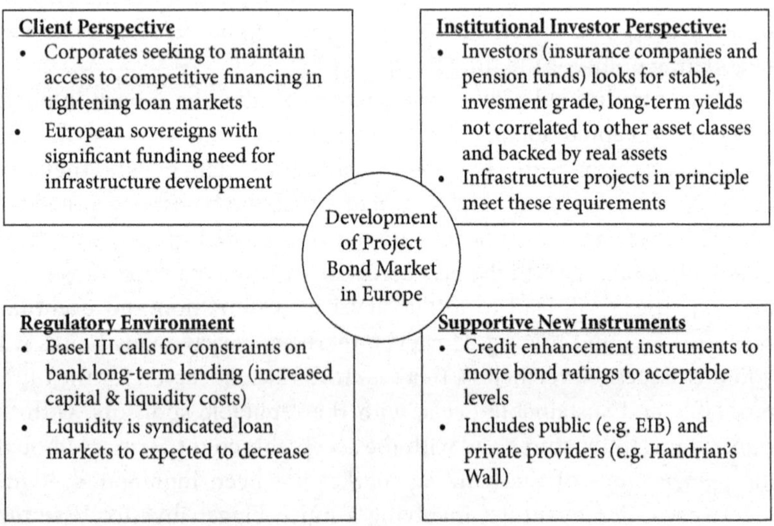

FIGURE 3.1 *Development of project bond market in Europe*

DOI: 10.1057/9781137524041.0008

Several features of bond financing should be taken into account when considering it as an option for financing infrastructure projects (EIB, 2012a):

- **Maturity/refinancing risk** – Bonds are by nature a long-term commitment and this feature permits perfectly matching institutional investors' long-term liabilities (pension funds, insurance companies) while also meeting PPP contract (concession agreement) maturities. Thus, it entails no refinancing risk comparing to short-term commercial bank loans.
- **Pricing** – In current market conditions, the total costs of bond financing often are comparable to the conventional bank lending costs, and a pricing advantage is envisaged in the near future due to the developments in the banking landscape described above. Such a pricing advantage could contribute to improving the value for money of a certain infrastructure project.
- **Credit quality** – Bond investors typically seek high quality assets in order to meet the regulation requirements and match their risk appetite profiles. To meet investors' expectations, the structuring arrangers for bond issues involve rating agencies to structure the transactions in a way to achieve a certain minimum acceptable rating ("A-"). Since typical PPP infrastructure project structures to achieve a "BB+" or "BBB" rating, bond financing is forced to involve "credit enhancing" instruments to meet the rating required by investors.
- **Transaction size** – Due to the bond financings' features such as high structuring/placement/legal costs, complexity and investor amount appetite, they are suitable for projects of a significant size (above EUR 100 mn).
- **Preparatory costs** – Bond financing involves significant preparatory costs. Bond solution financing requires more time to prepare than bank solutions as there is a need to obtain credit rating, prepare the bond placement documentation, market the bonds with investors and meet regulatory requirements.
- **Deliverability and pricing uncertainties** – The deliverability and pricing are usually resolved upon actual issuance meaning that some uncertainties inevitably remain throughout the procurement process. As a bond pricing is market-driven, the risk of price fluctuation between final offer and financial close will in most cases lie with the government (in PPP structure).

DOI: 10.1057/9781137524041.0008

- **Cost of carry** – Since the bond issued amount is typically drawn at once upon issuance, the sponsor will have to invest these proceeds until they are actually required within the project over its construction period. This normally results in a so-called "negative carry" because the short-term interest received is generally lower than the costs to the bondholders. This contrasts with conventional bank lending, where the drawdown profile is structured due to the construction period needs.
- **Financial covenants** –Bond transaction requirements are covenant lighter compared to loan financing where commercial banks requires larger number of financial pledges.
- **Termination provisions** – In case of early repayment, the bond terms will normally require a prepayment fee in addition to return on the amount outstanding.
- **Controlling creditor** – In traditional bank loans, during the project lifespan, the lenders have the opportunity to be directly involved in the management and monitoring of coordination. In case of bond financing, a controlling creditor needs to be appointed to manage the interest of the many bondholders.

3.3 Bank loan versus project bonds

The discussion of the alternative funding in infrastructure financing is a very important topic at the present time in the PF sector. In particular, the involvement of banks alongside project bonds can be beneficial in respect to effectively managing construction risk, negative carry, decision making and procurement because of the flexibility and active engagement that they can provide. There exists the optimism among banks that PF would continue playing a key role in the future transaction but realism might be different, mainly due to the practical and regulatory barriers.

In respect to bank loans, commercial banks and project sponsors intend to agree to try shifting the refinance risk to the public side (aiming at cheaper, albeit shorter, bank lending and better value for money concept). Nevertheless, this strategy, in every situation, is not very feasible and is rather dependent on several factors such as project country, stakeholders and type of a project and especially to a commercial banks business strategy. Therefore, typically, they need to bear the refinance risk in such a case.

DOI: 10.1057/9781137524041.0008

On the other side, we can expect that World Bank, EIB, ECAs and other multilateral agencies (EBRD, IFC) will continue to play a very important role in respect to financing infrastructure transactions even though tighter restrictions in terms of funds availability have been addressed also to them. Private investments will also continue to grow in importance. In addition, specialist funds may enter into the market; pension funds and sovereign wealth funds will increasingly look to invest in infrastructure project and companies as well.

Bankers are often commenting that the debt capital markets are unlikely to support a pure greenfield infrastructure project with no track record due to high construction risks which they do not want to bear. Furthermore, it is completely correct that in the past project bonds have been considered only as the refinancing instrument for existing project loans rather than financing the purely greenfield project. However, nowadays, with certain governmental and international financial institutions support, in terms of credit enhancement in the construction period, institutional investors are prepared to accept such projects if a proper credit rating grade has been assigned.

In Table 3.1, we can observe the main differences between bond and bank loan funding options, which will play the essential role in future decision making on which financing solution to undertake. The main highlighted aspects are maturity, interest (coupon) rate, refinancing risk, financial covenants and drawdown/repayment profile.

In conclusion, the governmental budget constraints for infrastructure sector expenditure along with reduced overall appetite of commercial banks to take and hold long-term project loan assets due to liquidity requirements by regulators are incentivizing alternative funding investors to offer their financing. However, in order to stay in the PF business, banks need to find an innovative way to access institutional money for their long-term infrastructure lending activities without using a balance sheet capacity. The international debt markets present a huge untapped pool of capital available for project financing. As we can realize, a project bond instrument is not a completely new phenomenon and it has been extensively deployed in infrastructure projects in Europe and the US in pre-financial crisis with an important difference – the involvement of monoline insurers, which have exited the market after the economic depression (Bradley, McLaren and Corlett, 2012). However, the institutional investors are still very cautious entering into the infrastructure transaction especially in the CEE market. Therefore, we are beginning

DOI: 10.1057/9781137524041.0008

TABLE 3.1 *Pros and cons of project bond solution versus bank loan*

Bonds	Bank debt
Longer maturity – may be cheaper, longer certainty of funding	Generally shorter tenor; refinancing risk
Fixed rate funds – benefit to financial model and no swap required	Typically floating rate finance; nevertheless, normally hedging with IRS
Investors do not want prepayment – focus on long-term yield	Generally greater prepayment flexibility (usually amortized loans)
Bondholders passive; hard to organize – less project "interference"	Relationship lenders
Difficult to modify terms	More flexibility – client driven mentality
Lighter covenants; less discretion	Heavily negotiated covenant package with closer monitoring
Default: trade out (no negotiations, sell out immediately when bondholders take a decision)	Default: typically workout (negotiating a new agreements between a troubled borrower and a lender)
One closing: no drawdowns	Less market risk; committed funding and drawdowns when required
Lower interest cost but "all in funding cost" should be considered swap costs, cost of carry, reserving/rating requirements, financial ratios and so on	Limited cost of carry
Ratings are vital; may have to pierce the sovereign ceiling	Ratings not normally required or obtained
Public disclosure, eventual listing	No public disclosure required

Source: Adapted from Bradley, McLaren and Corlett (2012).

to notice the governmental organization's credit supports programmes, which intend to foster the project bond market and establish a well-structured way for an alternative source of financing infrastructure projects in Europe.

In conclusion of this section, we move to briefly consider the cost of bond funding. Figure 3.2 shows us a lower average spread provided by bonds versus comparable PF bank loans in recent years. In this sense, we can expect that sponsors will try to access project bond issuance with which they will decrease their financial costs. Even though the gap is narrowing, the spread is still in favour of project bonds in 2013, 260 bps versus 170 bps, respectively. Here, we have another fact which plays in favour of project bonds when considering advantages and disadvantages.

DOI: 10.1057/9781137524041.0008

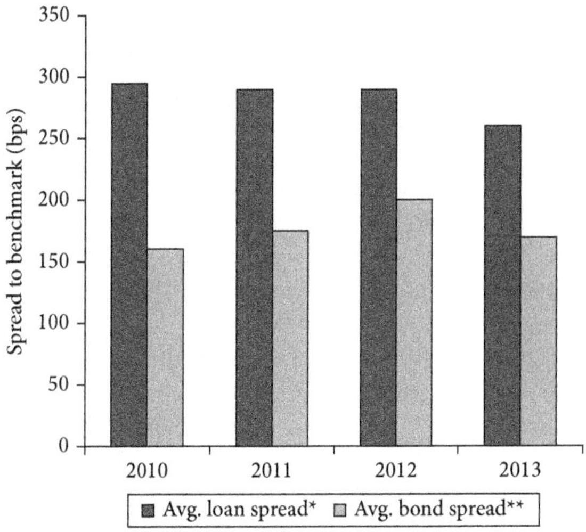

FIGURE 3.2 *Average spread on PF loans and comparable bonds*

Notes: Infrastructure sectors considered are water, transportation, power, oil and gas
* Spread over Euribor swap rate
** Spread over German Bund yields

Source: Our research on Thomson Reuters data source.

Notes

1 Negative carry is the situation in which the cost of holding a security exceeds the yield earned. An investor might, however, achieve a positive after-tax yield on a negative carry trade if the investment comes with tax advantages, as might be the case with a bond whose interest payments were non-taxable.

2 Cash sweep is the mandatory use of excess free cash flows to repay the outstanding debt rather than to distribute it to shareholders as dividends payments.

3 PEBBLE, launched in December 2012, stands for "Pan European Bank to Bond Loan Equitisation" and was intended to provide project bonds with credit enhancement through the provision of a subordinated cushion during the riskiest phase of a project (construction and ramp up). Whilst during this phase, the B Lenders, as commercial banks, control the project by responding to waiver and consent requests as controlling creditor. The SPV is funded with the following financing elements:

- Construction revolving facility, provided by commercial banks, is drawn to meet construction costs (against certificated value, in the normal way) and periodically refinanced by a combination of the A Notes and B Loan;

- A Notes are subscribed for by institutional investors on a fixed drawdown and amortization schedule and which rank senior to the B Loan; and
- B Loan (with its related hedging) provided by commercial banks, which ranks junior to the A Notes, but is scheduled to amortize in advance of the A Note principal repayments.

Hadrian's Wall Capital (HWC) was established in 2009 to provide a new market-based bond-financing solution to European infrastructure debt markets. The first transaction was announced in May 2012 with commitments from Aviva Life & Pensions UK, EIB and the Development Bank of Japan.

The HWC product offers debt to a borrower through a single debt instrument provided at a spread over the appropriate bond benchmark. HWC will then tranche the debt into two tranches, a senior tranche as A Notes and a subordinated tranche as B Notes. The A Notes are issued to the capital markets and the B Notes are placed with a fund. The fund, through the B Notes, will provide a "first loss" tranche of debt for a project. Typical funding proportions might be A Notes representing 75 per cent, B Notes representing 10 per cent and equity 15 per cent. The aim would be to take the total project debt with a rating of BBB-/BBB and use the fund to enhance the risk profile of the A Notes to at least BBB+. The structure employs the principle according to which the B Notes are the controlling creditor of the project unless the project performance falls below pre-defined thresholds, in which case the A Notes take control. This alleviates the need for bondholders to manage the project on a day to day basis unless the project is in distress.

DOI: 10.1057/9781137524041.0008

4

The Europe 2020 Project Bond Initiative

Abstracts: *The new instrument of the Project Bond Initiative (PBI) developed jointly by the EU and EIB was established with the aim of relaunching and revitalizing the project bond market in Europe, which reached a standstill in the aftermath of the financial crisis. Looking at its funding experience in transactions coming from Western Europe projects achieving the financial close during the initial pilot phase, we try to extract from the available case histories the main features and the best practices that have triggered the success for financing these projects so far.*

Rossi, Emanuele and Rok Stepic. *Infrastructure Project Finance and Project Bonds in Europe.* Basingstoke: Palgrave Macmillan, 2015.
DOI: 10.1057/9781137524041.0009.

4.1 General overview

The financial and economic crisis has significantly impacted the options for funding infrastructure projects, especially in Europe. As an answer to the current circumstances on the market, in 2012, the European Commission and EIB developed[1] an instrument that is intended to support the investment infrastructure gap, called the Project Bond Initiative (PBI).

EIB takes over a similar role as monoline insurers in PF transactions. However, in contrast to the monoliner involvement, which provided a full wrap to enhance the rating of the debt to "AAA" rating, the EIB will provide senior bond investors an additional safety net via injection of subordinated debt to lift the credit quality of the project bonds, depending on the project and sovereign risk. With PBI, the EIB will try to provide eligible infrastructure transactions with Project Bond Credit Enhancement (PBCE) in the form of a subordinated instrument and assume the risk of the given debt facility. The PBCE is a very unique product available in the European financial market, in terms of its open structure, tenor and execution team. We might say that it is perhaps the only option for many European projects, which are large and complex, to access debt capital markets due to the characteristics of private/institutional investors. Stakeholders consider the PBCE as a good use of EU funds, and it has a much higher multiplier effect than structural funds or other financial instruments, such as the Marguerite Fund.[2] The core benefit envisaged is the improvement of credit ratings of the senior bonds. PBCE would trigger the bond rating one to two notches higher, which is fundamental to bond pricing and locating investors' appetite for such an instrument. This lower financing cost in the project represents a saving for taxpayers and releases governmental budgets meaning that can be invested in other infrastructure needs. EIB wants to persuade institutional investors to participate in funding of infrastructure projects.

PBCE instruments provided by EIB can be a subordinated tranche in one of two possible forms:

- Funded PBCE (Figure 4.1): A funded subordinated debt. Cost overruns during construction cannot be absorbed.
- Unfunded PBCE (Figure 4.2): A contingent credit line for an already fully financed project, which is used in case of overrun in construction costs or if the income is insufficient to meet interest obligations.

DOI: 10.1057/9781137524041.0009

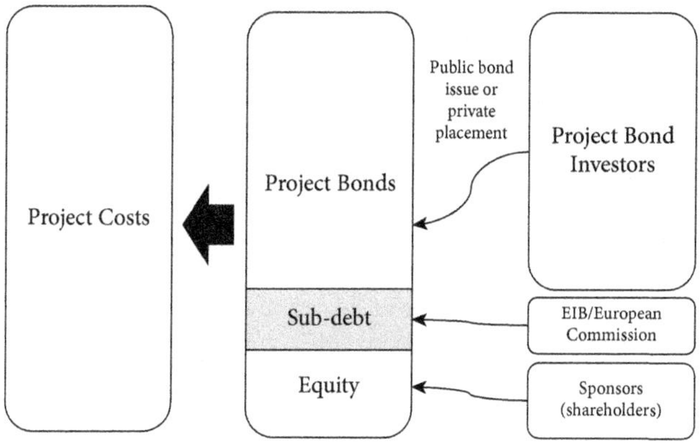

FIGURE 4.1 *Funded PBCE structure outlook*
Source: Adapted from EIB (2012a).

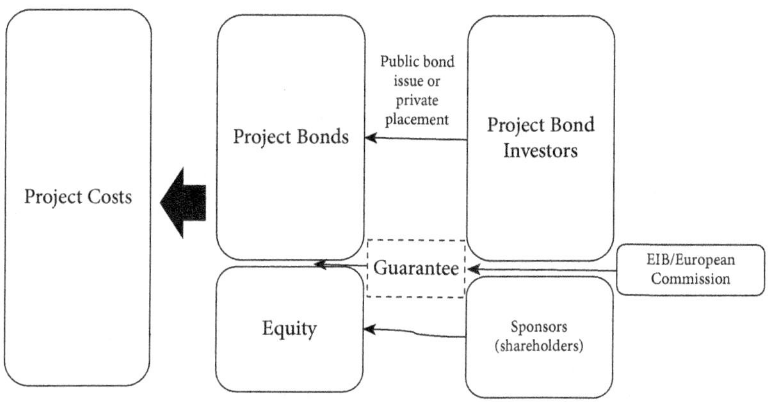

FIGURE 4.2 *Unfunded PBCE structure outlook*
Source: Adapted from EIB (2012a).

A comparison between the characteristics of these two different forms is also described in Table 4.1.

However, we have to distinguish the mechanism of PBCE from a monoline insurance company[3]:

a. A guarantee provided by PBCE does not cover the entire amount of bond issuance; the maximum size of PBCE available for a certain transaction is not above EUR 200 million or 20 per cent of the nominal amount of credit enhanced senior bond.

DOI: 10.1057/9781137524041.0009

TABLE 4.1 *Comparison between funded and unfunded PBCE*

	Funded PBCE (subordinated debt)	Unfunded PBCE (letter of credit)
Summary description	Decreases the required senior loan amount and consequently also increases the corresponding financial coverage	Contingent subordinated loan turning into funded subordination with the purpose of partial senior loan prepayment when financial performance drops beyond a certain DSCR trigger level or in case of liquidity/additional debt requirements during construction (also could act as a standard liquidity facility when replenished after the first drawing)
Completion risk	Rating neutral: Not increasing the amount of contingency	Rating positive: Support liquidity shortfall from delay, against cost overruns and so on
Operation and revenue risk	Rating positive: Increasing the senior loan facility ability to face reduction in CAFDS from revenue shock or cost jump	Rating positive: Usually no difference to the subordinated debt instrument
Infrastructure/renewal risk	Rating positive: Increasing flexibility to meet lifecycle costs/ongoing CAPEX programme and maintenance	Rating positive: Usually no difference to the subordinated debt instrument
Structural features	Rating neutral: No impact on liquidity position beyond higher debt service coverage	Rating neutral: When selectively drawn, it provides liquidity support, however, in case of automatic rebalancing, this may only happen after the facility has been at least partially exceeded after having been drawn in full previously – greater liquidity support is possible in structures where the rebalancing is not triggered automatically as bondholders may vote to selectively draw on the PBCE rather than rebalance in one go
Best suited for	Operating projects with lower expected cash flow fluctuation (Availability-based PPPs)	Greenfield projects and projects potentially exposed to uncertain events on revenues or costs (volume risk, technical outage)

Source: Authors' own research.

DOI: 10.1057/9781137524041.0009

b. As a subordinated instrument tool, PBCE is formed to improve the credit rating of the project bonds, not to extend EIB's AAA credit rating to the transaction.

The basic logic is that there are many long-term investors (pension funds, insurance companies) who are ready to invest for moderate returns and identifiable risk, whereby, major infrastructure investments share the same mentioned characteristics. The infrastructure deals mainly fail to be implemented due to governmental budget constraints. The instrument is designed to provide an alternative to financing projects by conventional bank lending or participation of governmental grants in order to minimize the infrastructure financing gap. If a project can be appropriately structured, grants and project bonds could potentially be combined.

To be eligible for the PBI, the following infrastructure project prerequisites are to be considered:

- Project quality is a key (technically and economically feasible)
- PBI is looking at those projects fulfilling specific sectorial eligibility criteria (motorways, healthcare, prisons, educational facilities, power, telecom)
- Involvement of EIB from very beginning of the project is essential
- Credit rating: investment grade limited
- Project stakeholder's structure (governmental participation as PPP structure)
- Requires bond market infrastructure
- Requires ring-fenced assets
- Robust financial structure prior to PBCE

The biggest challenge, we can currently foresee, is the adjustments of characteristics of PBI in a way to also be a suitable financing instrument for the CEE region, where the needs of infrastructure transactions are the highest, and proper due diligence is needed to assure the feasibility of the project. Furthermore, the initiative should particularly focus on sub-investment grade transactions, notably in countries where there is limited access to project finance debt. Besides that, many institutional investors have not set up internal infrastructure teams due to low numbers of investment made in the past, making them vulnerable from the due diligence point of view. PBCE will not really eliminate the need for that, but it should help to increase the confidence of investing in

DOI: 10.1057/9781137524041.0009

infrastructure projects and increase the flow of senior bonds simplifying and standardizing project structure (EIB, 2012a).

Also, it is worth mentioning that high political willingness by EU/EIB to implement PBCE and further develop the PBCE pipeline could be observed on the European market. There are several reasons for that. First one can be to reopen the debt capital markets to greenfield infrastructure post the decline of the monolines. Furthermore, the EU is aware of the importance of investment in infrastructure for further growth of the European Union, especially in the less-developed CEE. In late 2014, the new Investment Plan for Europe was launched by the new EU Commission, and it is seen as the last move toward the direction of infrastructure growth and improvement in Europe.

The launch of PBI 2020 has already played a positive role in stimulating discussion and in the development of alternative financing solutions from both the private and national governmental sector. The next stage, crucial in development, will be to match expenditure demands and to successfully complete the first stage pipeline of projects in order to provide best practices for the future.

4.2 Case studies – PBI 2020 pilot phase

The scope of the EIB's PBI pilot phase was to test the project bond concept and to identify advantages as well weaknesses the PBCE instrument would be facing when undertaken. The pilot phase started in November 2012 and is planned to finish at the end of 2016. The main PBI objectives, as mentioned above, are the following:

- Stimulation of investment in key strategic EU infrastructure in transport and energy market
- Establishment of debt capital market (DCM) as an alternative source of financing for infrastructure projects

During the pilot phase, nine infrastructure projects have been approved for refinancing through this risk sharing facility developed by the EU and EIB. Furthermore, much more will follow, as PBCE will probably be used to leverage the estimated EUR 315 billion of Investment Plan for Europe over the period 2015–17. The projects being chosen in the PBI pilot phase so far are the following:

DOI: 10.1057/9781137524041.0009

- Castor Gas Storage Spain (EUR 200 m)
- OFTO Greater Gabbard UK (GBP 46 m)
- A11 Motorway Belgium (EUR 115 m)
- Axione Telecom Infrastructure France (EUR 38 m)
- Autobahn A-7 PPP Germany (EUR 86 m)
- Passante di Mestre motorway, Italy, EUR 180 m
- N25 New Ross motorway, Ireland, EUR 50 m
- A45 motorway, France, EUR 150 m
- A7 – Phase 2, Germany, EUR 40 m

Out of those projects, the first five have already been signed with the PBCE instrument while the last four transactions have been only approved by EIB Board so far but not yet signed. In the next sections, we will comment more in detail on the selection of the more advanced stage projects, from which we will extract the most important issues and advantages.

4.2.1 Castor Gas Storage Spain

The first project under the EIB's PBCE initiative was Castor Gas Storage in Spain, with financial closing in September 2013 and a capacity to provide storage for 30 per cent of Spain's daily gas consumption. It has been the most notorious case of a project being refinanced by project bonds with the EIB PBI instrument. Table 4.2 gives us a transaction details description. We must highlight that it has also been the less successful project of the PBI pilot phase. One of the main reasons for that was a poor risk assessment and due diligence of environmental impact. After the first gas injections caused a series of earthquakes, the project had to be stopped. Due to a contractual definition, it was the Spanish government who had to take the losses caused by shutting down the storage. In June 2014, Fitch Ratings downgraded the Castor bonds from BBB+ to BB+, making them "non-investment grade" bonds, which consequently further decreased the trust amongst investors. Thus, the project is very likely to end in a massive government bailout by Spanish taxpayers.

The ESCAL (sponsors) received the approval for the relinquishment of the concession in October 2014 by the Spanish Ministry of Industry, Energy and Tourist. The Spanish government agreed to pay EUR 1.35 billion to the sponsors before 17 November 2014. At present, the EUR 200 m PBCE has not yet been called and will remain available until all senior bonds are discharged. In conclusion, we need to stress out that

DOI: 10.1057/9781137524041.0009

TABLE 4.2 *Transaction details of Castor Gas Storage Spain*

Project	Construction and operation of an underground gas storage and associated facilities providing storage for 30% of Spain's daily gas consumption
CAPEX	EUR 1.65 billion
Duration	30 years concession
Financial close	September 2013
Financial support	Project bond – EUR 1.4 billion Funded PBCE – EUR 200 million
Coupon	Fixed rate of 5.756% at a spread of 100 points of Spanish governmental bonds
Maturity date	December 2034
WALL	12.5 years
Rating	BBB (S&P)
Bond issuer	Watercraft Capital, an SPV based in Luxembourg
Bond investors	30 geographically diversified investors (Germany, France, Spain, Italy, UK and Luxembourg) with pension funds and insurance firms taking over 60% of the total amount, the remainder being agencies, fund managers and banks (only 4%). EIB bought EUR 300 m of the bonds.

Source: Authors' own research.

project bond financial mechanism by itself was not an issue; however, the proper due diligence could avoid the failure of the project.

4.2.2 OFTO Greater Gabbard UK

The Greater Gabbard offshore is the first UK based infrastructure project to attract finance from institutional investors through the PBCE instrument from PBI. Bonds with a value of GBP 305 million have been issued to finance the new transmission link to connect the 140-turbine wind farm off the Suffolk coast with the UK mainland electricity and have been successfully placed with a broad range of investors.

The OFTO License entitles the project company to own and operate the assets for a period of 20 years and in return receives availability-based revenues (stable cash flow). The tariff paid to the operator is RPI-linked, and 90 per cent of the revenue is guaranteed.

The EIB has supplied the project with a GBP 45.8 million guarantee, representing 15 per cent of the bond issued, as a credit support under the

DOI: 10.1057/9781137524041.0009

PBCE scheme that allows this specific project a one notch upgrade in the project's rating provided by Moody's. Under the PBCE (unfunded) model, additional liquidity will be provided for the project if required to allow enhanced recovery for senior lenders by reducing outstanding debt and act as a first loss piece in the financing structure. Furthermore, in Table 4.3, we cast an insight in the transaction details.

The successful public bond issued for the Greater Gabbard OFTO represents the first use of the EIB PBI in the UK. This brings a completely new dimension to infrastructure finance in the UK energy sector by attracting greater participation by institutional investors in an essential part of the offshore wind projects. This new scheme significantly supports investment to connect renewable energy to the national grid. The EIB is committed to supporting crucial energy investment across Europe and has provided more than GBP 6 billion for long-term investment in the UK energy sector over the last five years.

Successful completion of the Greater Gabbard OFTO transaction, the second PBI-PBCE deal (after Castor Gas Storage), shows the clear advantages of increasing engagement of institutional investors through a more attractive credit rating. This is the first deal under the Project Bond Initiative where the credit enhancement has been directly backed by the EU budget. Investor confidence is essential for reviving capital markets as key sources of finance for Europe's long-term infrastructure.

TABLE 4.3 *Transaction details of Greater Gabbard UK offshore wind facility*

Project	The OFTO License entitles the project company to own and operate the assets
Duration	30 years concession
Financial close	November 2013
Financial support	Equity – GBP 46 million Public bond – GBP 305 million Unfunded PBCE – GBP 45.8 million
Coupon	Fixed coupon of 4.137%
Maturity date	November 2032
Rating	A3 (Moody's)
Bond investors	Fund managers 78%, insurance companies and pension funds 22%
Project Company	OFTO project company is an equally shared joint venture between Balfour Beatty Investments, Equitix and AMP Capital Investors

Source: Authors' own research.

4.2.3 A11 Belgian motorway project

The A11 is the first transport project and the first greenfield PPP to reach financial closing through the EIB's PBCE scheme. It is also the first listed construction phase project bond in Europe.

Deutsche Bank is acting as the global coordinator in a EUR 577.9 million of senior-rated amortizing bonds priced at a fixed-rate coupon of 4.49 per cent. The note holders are Allianz Global Investors and the EIB. They subscribed to EUR 433 million, with the EIB acting as an anchor investor for EUR 145 million of the issuance. The bonds will be amortized gradually after the construction period. In addition, the EIB is also providing a subordinated credit facility (LCs) of EUR 115 million, which has improved the credit rating of the bonds by three notches, from Baa3 to A3. It can be concluded that EIB, with the unfunded PBCE instrument, helps to build a self-sustaining market by taking the subordinated debt in the capital structure to boost the performance of project bond tranches. In Table 4.4, we can see the characteristics of the transaction in more detail. Furthermore, in Appendix A.2, we can observe the transaction structure in detail and the relationships between parties involved.

As the first PBI 2020 greenfield project, the deal is using the innovative cost overrun mechanism, which is likely to be applied to future PBI deals. The credit enhancement availability during the construction period for any

TABLE 4.4 *Transaction details of Belgium A11 Motorway*

Issue Amount:	EUR 577.9 million
Issue Rating	A3 (Moody's)
CAPEX	EUR 700 million
Issue price:	100%
Coupon:	Fixed rate at 4.49%
Final Redemption date:	September 2045 (31.5 years)
Issuance date	20th March 2014
Status:	Secured amortizing bonds
Debt-to-Equity	88:12
Equity	EUR 80 million of shareholder loans and pure equity
ADSCR	1.25x
Global Coordinator:	Deutsche Bank
Book runners:	Deutsche Trustee is bond trustee and security trustee
Investors:	Allianz Global Investors (EUR 433 m) EIB (EUR 145 m)
PBCE	Letter of credit amounting to EUR 115.58 m (unfunded)

Source: Authors' own research.

DOI: 10.1057/9781137524041.0009

possible construction cost overruns is a significant mitigant for the institutional investor involved. Clearly, the project company should still first look for recourse against the normal parties and have a PBCE letter of credit as an available backup option. Moreover, despite the deferred payment structure, the credit enhancement is available from the issue date on.

This transaction is recognized as a transaction possessing very innovative financial features. The bond placement will feature a deferred drawdown profile over the construction period with monthly disbursements in order to provide better value for the sponsors (and mitigate negative carry). This delayed drawdown approach is enabled with forward bond purchase agreements,[4] which have recently emerged as a solution to the negative carry. Secondly, the transaction is structured as committed financing proving that the project bond investor base has matured to the point that they can assess and understand construction risk, negative carry and fulfil the monitoring function.

In addition, the bond is structured as a secured amortized bond meaning that the financing solution possesses a scheduled redemption plan, which is enabled by combined issue of bonds and partly paid notes.[5] As we know, notes are issued in two, three, five and ten-year terms. Conversely, bonds are long-term investments with terms of more than ten years. Due to those characteristics, the transaction can afford the gradually amortized profile through its operational period.

There exists a predefined amortization profile (scheduled redemption) for a bond, which is described in the project agreement. In the scheduled redemption of the bonds, the bonds are redeemed in instalments on each payment date. Since there was an issue of notes as well, which possess the maturities up to ten years, they are repaid first to the investors (in the first ten years) and afterwards starts principal repayment of long-term bonds, which have maturity up to 31.5 years.

Nevertheless, PBI includes the concept of a controlling creditor, giving recommendations on amendments, consents and waivers on behalf of bondholders and in this way, provides an effective decision-making procedure without disenfranchising bondholders (InfraNews, 2014). Early involvement of EIB in the transaction further helps in mitigating any perceived deliverability risk in pursuing a bond financing option during the procurement.

In conclusion, Belgian motorway financing has sent several signals that the project bond sector in Europe has moved past its post-crisis structural issues and is now ready to take on new challenges in public sector

DOI: 10.1057/9781137524041.0009

support. The overall impression of the A11 closing in Belgium is that EU driving forces made the bond solution happen despite the aggressive bank pricing. However, the bond's competitive pricing is a milestone in proving the PBI initiative can pass the deliverability test. The Belgium A11 deal is known as one that has delivered great value for money.

4.2.4 A7 Autobahn PPP Germany

The project concerns the extension of motorway between the Bordesholm junction in Schleswig-Holstein and the Hamburg Nordwest junction. During the construction period, traffic will be maintained. Capacity expansion in this important European corridor will cancel out a traffic bottleneck. By speeding up traffic flow and improving safety along this key economic artery, this project will make a significant positive contribution to the economy. The PPP scheme being part of the project makes a decisive contribution to its positive impact. Therefore, the project company is paid on the basis of availability payments (stable cash flows). The fee depends chiefly on the extent and quality of the road section made available for use by motorists. In case of the motorway being non-compliant to the pre-agreed conditions, certain deductions are made on availability payment amounts.

The total financing is up to EUR 770 million. It consists of senior bonds, privately placed to institutional investors purchasing senior bonds successively during the four-year construction period to mitigate negative carry as already explained in the A11 transaction section. EIB's PBCE serves to mitigate potential cost overruns and short-term bank debt for bridge financing of milestone payments pursuant to construction progress and several shareholder loans from the sponsors. The PBCE guarantee instrument enables the senior bonds to achieve a rating of A3 from Moody's (stand-alone rating of Baa2). The combination of project bond and EIB PBCE with milestone bridge facilities led to challenging intercreditor issues.[6] In Table 4.5, we can observe the transaction details and notice that the coupon rate is very favourable as well as the debt-to-equity ratio.

In any case, the A7 is still bearing certain issues and is unlikely to silence the critics. We can see that the EIB has used its credit enhancement instrument mostly on projects located in stable environment and with strong credit backup. Hence, EIB is not bearing a large proportion of risk but charging a high interest for its facility available in the transaction.

It is clear that the enhancement by EIB was enough to allow the A7's sponsors to attract institutional investors in the very early stage of the

DOI: 10.1057/9781137524041.0009

TABLE 4.5 *Transaction details of A7 Autobahn in Germany*

Project	Construction of PPP road and it is scheduled to be completed by the end of 2018
Construction costs	EUR 770 million
Duration	30 years concession
Financial close	August 2014
Financial support	Equity – EUR 90 million Project bond – EUR 430 million Unfunded PBCE – EUR 90 million (20% of senior bonds) Bridge loan – 82 million
Debt-to-Equity	90:10
Coupon	Fixed coupon at 2.96%
Maturity date	September 2034
Rating	A3 (Moody's) – stand-alone credit quality of the project during construction Baa2
Bond investors	Institutional investors from US, Canada and Europe (AXA, KfW IPEX, MassMutual, Aegon, ING, Sun Life and EIB)
Bond issuer	Via Solutions, the SPV selected last June by Germany's Federal Ministry of Transport and Digital Infrastructure as the preferred bidder for the PPP

Source: Authors' own research.

transaction and encourage them to offer delayed drawdowns. Besides that, the PBCE enabled the lift of the bonds' rating into A3 grade, which represents the comfort zone for European institutional investors. Clearly, for these developments alone, the product has proved its usefulness.

4.3 Case studies' findings

The pilot phase of the PBI plays a very important role for the future success of the initiative. The following findings can be drawn from the transactions' experience so far:

- **Liquidity**: There is clearly place in a market for project bonds being part of PBI, especially with interest from pension funds, insurance companies or specialised funds. Project bonds can perfectly match long-term liabilities with long-term assets and increase their yields. The raised debt financing through the bond issue is significant and demonstrates the level of liquidity for infrastructure projects.

DOI: 10.1057/9781137524041.0009

- **Private/institutional investor base:** We can observe high interest especially from UK, German and Benelux investors in the financing of large infrastructure assets across the Europe.
- **Credit rating advantage:** The bonds issued at non-investment grade, with credit enhancement facility, always gain two to three notches to bring the instrument to the investment grade and as a result, big interest from the investors (as well those with certain regulations).
- **Sovereign rating:** Few projects achieved a credit rating above the sovereign rating. This is very important for the future perspective of other infrastructure projects, which may take place in economies with non-investment grade rating. This confirms that financing can be found for even projects with riskier profiles, with appropriate credit enhancement and risk allocation.
- **Risk sharing and mitigation:** A large part of success can be allocated to the PBCE instrument, which absorbs a big part of construction risk.
- **Innovative feature in project bond financing:** This includes deferred drawdown profile, forward purchase agreements, amortization plan, and PBCE tool.

Amongst wider effects of the PBI pilot phase, we clearly need to consider the positive spillover on the overall infrastructure project bond market. The increased focus triggered by PBI instrument on infrastructure debt market financing has led to a sharp rise in other project bond issues compared to pre-PBI years. More significantly, the EIB reports that in 2013 bond financing has reached up to a 22 percentage of all project debt financing in the EU-28 against an average as low as 4 per cent in the 2000–12 period (EIB, 2013). This finding is quite impressive and very promising.

On the other hand, in the period between 2007–13, more than 90 per cent of bonds issued, in terms of volumes, were just refinancing, mainly brownfield projects, with a minority represented by greenfield investments. In this sense, there is still a lot of catching up to do in terms of the riskier segment of the greenfield projects.

4.4 Structural issues of the initiative

After observing the lesser performing of the PBI projects, it appears to us that projects have revealed some of the structural weaknesses of the project bond guarantee mechanism.

DOI: 10.1057/9781137524041.0009

Firstly, PBI is structured in way that the public entity (government) bears most of the risk in order to attract private investors meaning that losses are absorbed by taxpayers while profits are privatized. Moreover, the mechanism enables refinancing projects that failed to attract investments in any other way and as a result the risk of failure, may increase the public debt. Secondly, the transparency could be a huge concern. Despite very well and carefully managed documentation that took place, more detailed information about the contractual agreement, clauses and absorbed risk was not always clear.

However, despite these few issues, the EIB's project bonds process has continued to play a key funding role in UK OFTE Gabbard offshore wind project in late 2013. Furthermore, in 2014, two new transactions have benefited by PBI financial structure, greenfield A11 Belgium motorway project and A7 German motorway expansion, where institutional investors, who would not otherwise consider the deals, were not lacking. Also, the entire European PF financial community appears to be enthusiastic about and fully supports PBI. So far, one immediate conclusion can be drawn that EIB-backed project bonds, given the extent to which they are set up, not only favour but also cushion major investors and may well, in the short-term, trigger increased level of interest for any project that the EIB prefers to favour and prioritize.

4.5 Concluding remarks

After the analysis of transactions involved in the PBI scheme until now, we briefly summarize few conclusions which could improve the viability of the initiative and overcome certain issues which are still in place.

The PBCE instrument implementation should be flexible depending on each separate transaction's features. The guarantee facility (PBCE) percentage to total senior project bond amount should not be limited to EUR 200 million or 20 per cent. In our opinion, EIB can afford to bear more risk in larger or more complex transactions and in this way be released to certain extent public exposure. In such cases, the due diligence process should be managed by EIB as well what would improve the project risk assessment. The proportion guarantee/sub-debt should be allowed to decrease in the operational phase, once construction has been fully completed and the associated risks no longer persist. Also, for

DOI: 10.1057/9781137524041.0009

the operational period, bond investors could purchase a put option to exit the PBI, if it is no longer deemed necessary. One of the most important recommendations provided by many observers concerns the EIB acting as the first loss provider. In such cases, the EIB would much easier manage the intercreditor conflicts. There can perhaps be an evaluation process prior to pursuing the senior role as to whether it is vital to the deal as well as whether it is consistent with the EIB's broader investment policy objectives. This would also improve the ability of the instrument to absorb potential losses arising from changing market environment and sector specific developments.

In conclusion, we must also highlight that the PBI has had a wide catalytic effect in promoting capital market financing and institutional investors participation from a general project bond market perspective. Compared to pre-PBI years, the project bond market in Europe is no longer stagnant, and institutional investment has become a key feature of the market.

Notes

1 PBI has been set up by Regulation (EU) No. 670/2012 of the European Parliament and of the Council published on 31 July 2012 (*Official Journal of the European Union* L.204/1).

2 The Marguerite Fund is a pan European equity fund that acts as a catalyst for key investments in renewables, energy and transport.

3 Monoline insurance company gives investors and issuers the confidence to participate in the market by providing liquidity in a form of financial protection. For example an insurance company guarantees scheduled payments of interest and principal on a bond or other security in the event of a payment default by the issuer of the bond or security.

4 Forward bond purchase agreement is a contract between two private parties that establishes a bond transaction in the future at a predetermined price. In the transaction, a portion of the bonds (the initial issue bonds) will be subscribed and paid for on the issue date by the bond purchasers. The remaining portion of the bonds so-called "forward purchase bonds" will be subscribed and paid on the issue date and then will be repurchased by the issuer and transferred to bond custodian to be held for and on behalf of the issuer. Pursuant to the bond purchase agreement, the original bond purchasers shall subscribe and pay for the initial bonds on the issue date at a purchase price equal to 100 per cent of the principal amount of the initial issue bonds. The forward purchase bonds will be subscribed and paid for by the lead

DOI: 10.1057/9781137524041.0009

arranger on the issue date at a purchase price equal to 100 per cent of the principal amount of the forward purchase bonds. Immediately, following the purchase of the forward purchase bonds by the lead arranger, the issuer shall repurchase the forward purchase bonds on the issue date at the price equal to 100 per cent of the principal amount of the forward purchase bonds and the lead arranger shall transfer the bonds to the bond custodian (for and on behalf of the issuer). The proceeds received by the issuer, on the issue date from the subscription proceeds for the initial issue bonds and from the bond purchasers on each bond purchase date, will be applied by the issuer to fund the project costs and others fees of the issuer. Certain bond purchasers will purchase certain of the forward purchase bonds on each bond purchase date in accordance with the terms of an agreement between the issuer and the bond purchasers. This is the model which enables a gradual supply of liquidity to the project.

However, with the mentioned financing structure including forward purchase agreements, additional risk for the project company could arise. In case an investor who signed the forward purchase agreement fails to purchase the forward purchase bonds on any bond purchase date, the issuer may be unable to sell the corresponding forward purchase bonds to another purchaser at the same price. If the issuer can only sell them in the market at a lower price, there may be insufficient funds to complete the project in accordance with the requirements of the project agreement.

5 Partly paid notes are those notes whose principal amount may be increased up to a specified amount in accordance with certain terms and conditions.

6 Intercreditor issue addresses the problem of how banks might enforce their rights in the event of a default.

DOI: 10.1057/9781137524041.0009

5
Case Studies in CEE

Abstracts: *The empirical European market evidence shows how the project bonds, as an alternative financing solution in certain infrastructure projects, can play an important role.*

The case studies discussed come from the CEE region. Since the whole pilot phase of PBI has been implemented exclusively in Western Europe countries so far, we analyse the conditions that can sustain successful project bond issuance in CEE countries.

In particular, the Slovakia case is deemed to be the example of an emerging market being more ready to experiment with project bond issuance, where the EIB Project Bond Credit Enhancement scheme could be helpful and work very well.

Rossi, Emanuele and Rok Stepic. *Infrastructure Project Finance and Project Bonds in Europe.* Basingstoke: Palgrave Macmillan, 2015.
DOI: 10.1057/9781137524041.0010.

 DOI: 10.1057/9781137524041.0010

5.1 Introduction

In this chapter, we will confront the option of EIB supporting projects with PBI in the CEE region. From our research, the most credible country in which such an option is viable is Slovakia. Considering the facts that in late 2013 there was a refinancing of the R1 Motorway project with project bonds, and we have witnessed a large success, we assume that is very likely EIB will enter into one of the transactions in the form of a PBCE scheme. As we can see in Table 5.1, which is a pipeline extract from the EIB report (EIB, 2013) in respect to the PBI 2020, one of the potential projects approved and planned for PBCE option is a potential motorway financing in Slovakia. Our best guess would be that this project refers to the D4 Motorway. To conclude, our main assumption will be based on this strong indication. The involvement of the PBCE instrument by EIB in the potential financing structure makes a bond option a viable funding solution.

Thus, we will first analyse the R1 Motorway project in detail and see what characteristics are necessary to attract a large number of institutional investors to participate in bond purchases. Also, we will review all the advantages, which talks in favour of project bonds in Slovakian market. Later on, we will demonstrate the case of the envisaged D4 Motorway project and set up our assumptions to show that the PBI scheme is very suitable for this project. We will confront the project bond option with bank loans and show the advantages of bonds over loans, after running all the assumptions in a financial model.

Since the whole pilot phase of PBI has been applied only in Western Europe countries so far, we believe that Slovakia is an example of an emerging market where the PBCE scheme by EIB would work perfectly. We claim this after analysing several facts described throughout the present chapter.

TABLE 5.1 *Pipeline of EIB approved projects with PBCE option*

Type	Sector	Country	PBCE option in EUR million
TEN-T	Motorway	Germany	120
TEN-T	Motorway	UK	200
TEN-E	Grid connection to several offshore wind farms	UK	150
TEN-E	Gas storage	Italy	200
TEN-T	Motorway	Slovakia	200
TEN-E	Grid connection to several offshore wind farms	Germany	170

Source: EIB (2013, p.7)

DOI: 10.1057/9781137524041.0010

5.2 The Slovakian case

Slovakia's economic outlook looks quite positive. Despite some weaknesses, Slovakia's macroeconomic strength should allow it to maintain a favourable outlook in the medium term taking into account investment grade rating and a resilient banking system, solid and continued growth in 2013 and 2014 and other advantages for foreign investors.

At present, there is a considerable amount of liquidity in Slovakia from different financing sources:

- Abundant liquidity in the financial market:
  - In 2009, R1 Motorway project was closed amid the financial crisis and successfully raised around EUR 1 bn of bank debt.
  - In 2010, the banking market showed the same appetite for a new motorway project, raising EUR 1.3 bn of bank debt, but the deal was cancelled because the Slovak government decided not to grant a further extension; therefore, the PPP collapsed.
  - There is currently considerable appetite from the bank market to provide long-term debt for well-structured PPP deals in creditworthy countries.
- Strong appetite from the public bond markets was seen on the very successful refinancing of the R1 Motorway with an unwrapped project bond of EUR 1.2 billion in 2013.

The track record of project bonds could indicate the same interest from bond investors for the envisaged D4 Motorway project. Certainly, with involvement of a strong sponsor group and a bankable robust financial structure, we can expect a relatively high appetite. In addition, multilaterals such as EIB or other financial institutions, with innovative supporting instruments involved with investors from the debt capital market, should be able to complement any funding provided by commercial banks.

Alternative debt funding solutions such as unwrapped and wrapped (with financial guarantee insurance) bonds now allow access to different, more liquid classes of bond investors and provide further competitive tension to conventional debt solutions:

- Public bonds target the broadest investors' pool and are beneficial for maintaining pricing tensions when raising large debt amounts.
- Private placements are better suited for transactions which introduce structural complexity (e.g. delayed drawdowns) and with smaller issuance sizes.

DOI: 10.1057/9781137524041.0010

Furthermore, as we can observe in Figure 5.1, EIB's presence has a large track record in Slovakia from different sectors so far. This is a favourable indication for EIB's further engagement in Slovakia and the region, which will serve for our later financial structure assumptions. There seems to be a growing level of acceptance amongst investment funds aimed toward CEE and Slovakia region of what key characteristics the asset class should have for being considered as an institutional investor attractive proposition.

5.2.1 Appetite for project bonds in Slovakia

Project bond issuance is slowly penetrating into CEE as infrastructure programmes are looking into the capital markets to supplement or combine to conventional bank financing, which is being hit by tighter regulation in the region. Moreover, issuers are adopting a number of different funding structures, leading to different credit rating grades, which play an important factor for determining the financial costs of the project.

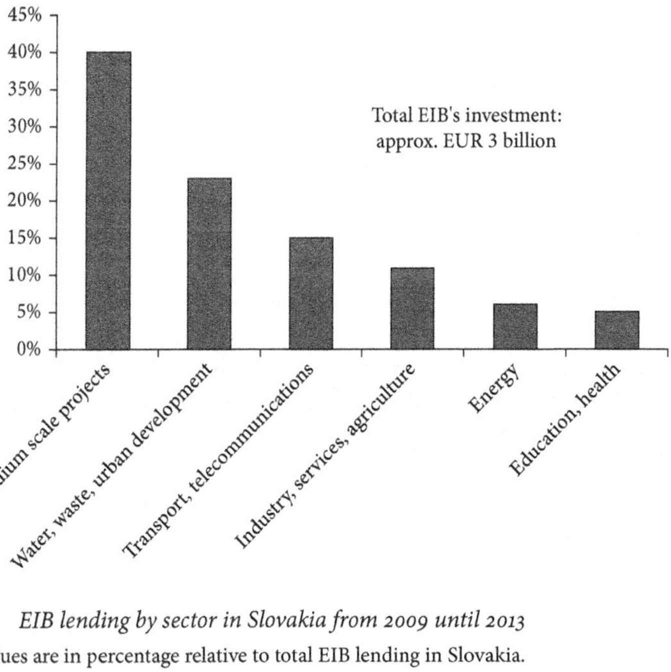

FIGURE 5.1 *EIB lending by sector in Slovakia from 2009 until 2013*

Notes: All values are in percentage relative to total EIB lending in Slovakia.

Source: Our research on EIB data source.

DOI: 10.1057/9781137524041.0010

The much more powerful and efficient way to assure sustained infrastructure investments is to determine the right regulatory framework and then for governments to keep away from implementing frequent short-term changes to the regulatory framework or introducing ad hoc taxation that weakens confidence on the part of investors. On that matter, lately, Slovakia has done a good job, clearly improving in terms of capital market legislation and macroeconomic market conditions. Apart from that, PPP regulatory framework is becoming more transparent and favourable to the sponsors. The latter changes provide several conditions for (bond) investors to recognize the country and its opportunities as a good investment. With regards to project bonds, the most relevant events in Slovakia are:

- Sovereign credit risk improvements
- Regulatory guidelines with regards to project bonds
- Clarification of the PPP framework and its alignment with the government budget

As a consequence of the above changes in Slovakia, the first project bond refinance of a PPP transaction (R1 Motorway) has been successfully structured in late 2013. The investment grade rating of BBB+/stable has attracted the attention of many institutional investors to be part of the transaction. The fact that the project is backed by availability payments by the Slovak government made to the sponsor allowed the obtained bond credit rating grade, which when combines with the track record of motorway deals and their behaviour, suits bond investors perfectly. This bond will establish a benchmark for other PPP projects in the region. Therefore, the institutional investors' confidence has significantly increased, making them prepared to invest in infrastructure PF deals as a bond investor. This also explains the changing behaviour of investors, being more and more prepared to bear the construction risk of a greenfield project clearly under certain protection mechanisms well defined in the concession and PPP agreement.

In addition, looking into the recent trend of the sovereign credit risk of the Slovakia Republic in the scope of institutional investors' requirements, it makes an excellent starting point for a new project bond financing in the region. Since the latest Slovakian sovereign credit risk is rated A (see Table 5.2), it implies that the project bond for a well-structured viable infrastructure PPP project could be easily reach a BBB- grade,

DOI: 10.1057/9781137524041.0010

TABLE 5.2 *Long-term Slovakia Republic Sovereign credit rating*

	Date of rating	Rating	Outlook
Standard & Poor's	01.08.2014	A	Positive
Fitch Ratings	15.11.2013	A+	Stable
Moody's	04.10.2013	A2	Stable

Source: Authors' own research on Thomson Reuters data source.

which is very acceptable from institutional investors. Furthermore, the Slovak Republic is a country which has a great perspective for the growing appetite amongst pension funds and insurance companies for diversification of their portfolio, and they additionally increase their returns with infrastructure assets investments compared to low yield governmental bonds, which dominates their portfolios.

5.2.2 Potential institutional investors

Based on the analysis of the European bond market and Slovakian capital market, a new bond transaction in Slovakia would attract a wide range of investors across the European investment grade space, including:

- Typical buyers of EUR Investment Grade bonds;
- Central and Eastern European/Emerging Markets focused investors;
- Infrastructure and project finance focused investors;
- High quality institutional investors looking for long dated assets, such as Euro based insurance companies and pension funds.

Figure 5.2 and Figure 5.3 show the detailed breakdown of the R1 Motorway refinancing bond investors profile by country and by type of investor, respectively. Thus, this case will serve as a benchmark for defining the expected potential investor base for the envisaged D4 Motorway transaction in Slovakia in 2015.

The main drivers of the transaction were institutional investors, who accounted for 51 per cent of allocations, followed by banks (24 per cent), multilaterals (16 per cent) and hedge/mutual funds managers (9 per cent). Geographically, the transaction was highly diversified: 34 per cent was purchased by German investors, followed by UK investors at 24 per cent and a domestic bid was around 11 per cent.

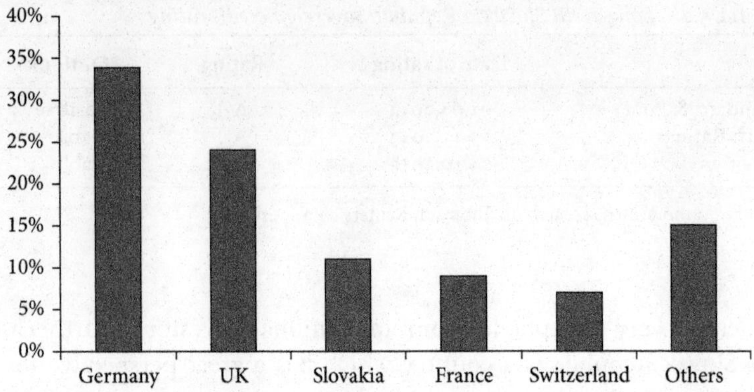

FIGURE 5.2 *Investors by country distribution – Slovakia R1 Motorway Bond Refinancing*

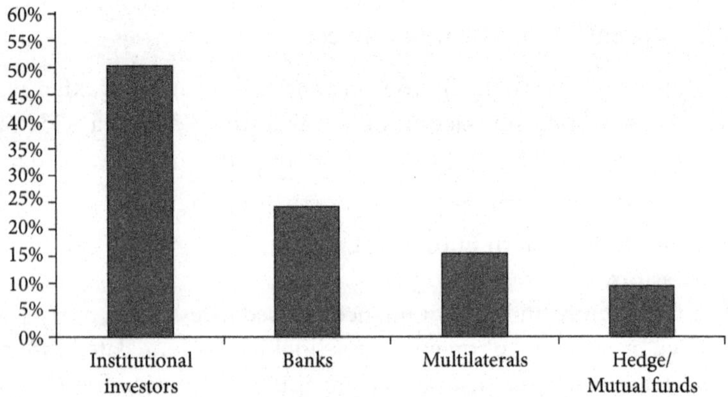

FIGURE 5.3 *Investors by type distribution – Slovakia R1 Motorway Bond Refinancing*

5.2.3 Slovakia R1 Motorway project deal refinancing

R1 Motorway was the first PPP road project in the Slovak Republic and is the result of a concession agreement signed in 2009 between the project company (owned 50 per cent by Vinci Concessions and 50 per cent by Meridiam Infrastructure) and the Ministry of Transport, Construction and Regional Development of the Slovak Republic. Appendix A.3 shows the detailed project contractual stakeholders' structure.

DOI: 10.1057/9781137524041.0010

The risk profile is based on availability fee payments; therefore, there is no demand risk component. Total project costs amount to around EUR 1.25 billion, financed by a mix of senior debt (EUR 981 million), shareholder funds (EUR 149 million) and internal generated cash (EUR 125 million per annum, indexed). Revenues for the project company come from the availability fee paid by the government.

The borrower was seeking to refinance the existing senior debt in 2013 due to the beneficial interest rate conditions. The purpose of accessing the capital markets was to significantly extend maturities, where final maturity after tough negotiations reached 12 years and also decreased interest expenses. For R1, the market conditions at that time were of great contribution to raise a targeted amount of approximately EUR 1.2 billion. A substantial part of the potential refinancing gain was passed on to the government in line with the concession agreement. This gain was materialized through improved robustness for the project company, more fluid yield for the shareholders, and enhanced value for money for the government. In addition, through the refinancing, the project company created value based on a stable long-term cash flow generated by the operation of the expressway while optimizing its financial costs, which benefitted from a more attractive project risk profile following the successful completion of the construction and start of the operation.

To minimize cost and expand the investor base for the transaction, banks were targeting an A-/BBB+ rating in order to meet several factors, which determined the rating of the issuer, including rating of the state entity making the availability based payments, the complexity and perceived risk of operating the road, availability of "bankable" business interruption insurance, the experience of the operator and the coverage ratios. Anyone of these factors did "constrain" the rating of the bond. However, the key factor was that the company had control over the financial coverage ratios, and therefore, a large part of feasibility was to optimize the relationship between financial coverage ratios, rating and pricing to arrive at the optimal refinancing NPV. The banks access to sub-debt infrastructure investors and the senior management of Europe's major insurers facilitated the whole transaction structuring.

Furthermore, EBRD acted as an anchor investor in refinancing of R1 Motorway with a subscription of EUR 200 million in a private placement of the project bond issued. This particular act by EBRD triggered overall reputation improvement and attracted a big pool of investors to participate in the bond purchase.

DOI: 10.1057/9781137524041.0010

In Table 5.3 and Table 5.4, we can see the comparison between financing conditions and other important features of the senior loan facility and project bond refinancing facility, respectively. It is clear that the conditions included in the project bond refinancing facility are much more favourable since the margins in bank loan have a step up scheme, thus refinancing was necessary. Secondly, with repayment extension and financial covenants more liberal, shareholders got more space for receiving dividends on regular basis. With project bonds, Slovakia has attracted many institutional investors, who will stay more active in the market. In this way, Slovakia did a very good advertisement for its financial market.

In conclusion, the use of project bonds in the refinancing structure was the preferred option by the borrowers due to several facts. First of all, there was no construction risk that has facilitated the suitable investment rating obtained for investors and consequently determined a lower coupon rate to what could be offered by commercial banks. In addition, the involvement of EBRD as an anchor investor made the transaction even more bond suitable and feasible. In that time, bank willingness to provide infrastructure refinancing with an extremely long tenor (25 years) and with such significant amount (EUR 1.2 billion) was rather low

TABLE 5.3 *Terms and conditions of the senior term loan facility before refinancing Slovakia R1 Motorway*

Amount	EUR 981 million
Purpose	To finance the Project Costs (excluding VAT) during construction
Maturity	28 years and 3 months
Margins (over IRS rate)	325bps until year 5 350bps until year 8 375bps until year 10 300bps from year 10 onwards/450bps if not refinanced
Arrangement Fee	330bps
Commitment Fee	50% of margin
Agency Fee	EUR 140k per annum
Drawdown	Pro rata to equity
Base Case Ratio	Min ADSCR. 1.25x Min LLCR. 1.30x
Default Ratio	Min ADSCR. 1.10x Min LLCR. 1.15x

Source: Authors' own research.

DOI: 10.1057/9781137524041.0010

TABLE 5.4 *Transaction details of Slovakia R1 Motorway refinancing with project bonds*

Issuer	GRANVIA A.S.
Issue Rating	BBB+ (S&P)
Issue Size	EUR 1.2 billion
Maturity Date	30 September 2039 (25 years 8 months)
Coupon	4.781%.
ADSCR	1.27x
Debt-to-Equity ratio	89:11
Sole arranger	Deutsche Bank
Joint Book runners	Deutsche Bank, Natixis
Advisers	Deutsche Bank (fin. adviser to the issuer) HSBC (fin. adviser to the grantor) Linklaters (legal adviser to the sponsor) Allen & Overy (bookrunner's legal adviser)

Source: Authors' own research.

in Slovakia. Also, with the project bond solution, we can avoid certain PF covenants and strict dividend restrictions, bringing another advantageous point for sponsor to undertake the bond solution.

5.2.4 Envisaged D4 Motorway project in Slovakia

During 2014, the Slovakian Ministry of Transport was considering whether to procure a 20 km bypass around Bratislava via the PPP route. At the beginning of 2015, the government decided to proceed with a real plan to structure D4 as PPP scheme project. The Ministry of Transport expects to reach the closing of the concession agreement in late 2015. The project was previously set to be funded by the state budget in 2011. However, the Slovakia's burgeoning deficit has limited those ambitions.

We believe that the D4 Motorway is particularly interesting to the private sector due its strong traffic forecasts. While the PPP option is still being considered by the Bratislava regional authorities, it is understood that one PPP option could involve the private partner collecting and retaining toll fees, dispensing with state-backed availability payments.

A tender for technical, legal and economic advisers for the project are being prepared, and the ministry expects that the tender for the concessionaire can start in 2015. Once the adviser is selected, the construction work is planned to begin. The project is being procured under the

DOI: 10.1057/9781137524041.0010

country's PPP framework and is expected to cost EUR 1.2 billion, with construction starting between 2015 and 2016.

In Figure 5.4, we can see the three most likely applied financing structures scenarios for a project of the characteristics possessed by D4 Motorway.

In option 1, the project company acquires a short-term loan, with maturity matching at least the construction period; later on, it refinances their primary bank facility by issuance of project bonds as we have seen in the R1 Motorway transaction in Slovakia. In this way, they avoid selling the construction risk to institutional investors, who do not usually accept due to not knowing how to assess it adequately.

In option 2, the company issues a bond from the very beginning of the project as we have seen in the case of A11 transaction in Belgium. The main two things that could differentiate between the bond financing solutions are the drawdown and repayment profile as well as the final maturity. As already mentioned, in our project bond scenario, we will use the innovative features of deferred drawdowns, using forward purchase agreements and an amortizing repayment profile with back loaded repayments.

In option 3, banks provide a term loan with a certain tenor, however, not matching the required maturity by the sponsor. When the term loan matures, the involved banks may refinance this loan by a new loan. The interest rate at which the banks lend under a new facility depends on the market conditions at that time, meaning that the sponsor bears a

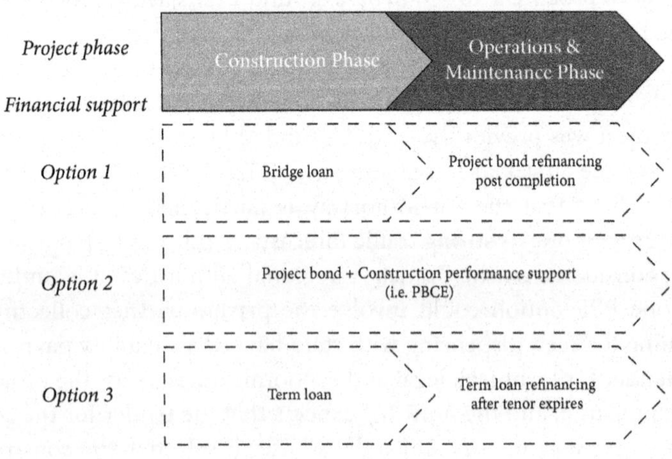

FIGURE 5.4 *Potential financing structure options for D4 Motorway transaction*

DOI: 10.1057/9781137524041.0010

refinancing risk including an interest rate risk as well due to the uncertainty of future interest rates on the capital markets. If feasible, banks normally offer an improved interest rate for the refinancing compared to the previous loan as the project has become up and running with a well-established track record. Additionally, the banks earn a portion of their profits from new fees for arranging the facility and for other banking services like cash management.

For our purposes, the most relevant options are clearly the second and the third ones as the first solution is substantially a replication of the funding strategy we discussed earlier in the R1 Motorway project case. For this reason, we will focus on and compare only the other two solutions in the following simulation exercise.

Assumptions and financial model

Starting with a simulation scenario on the two different prospective funding solutions discussed before (Option 2 and 3 in Figure 5.4), we need a financial model. The role of a financial model is simply to illustrate hypothetical results that are formally derived from specified assumptions. The aim is to evaluate ex ante the expected results of different funding strategies in order to reach the optimal choice from the sponsor point of view. In particular, the financial model applied to this kind of funding decision needs to focus on cash flows available for debt service (CFADS), which is the most relevant variable for all stakeholders involved in the deal. Meanwhile, the revenues, operating, maintenance and capital costs, interest rates and taxes can be modelled in alignment with the benchmark examples (A11, A7 and R1) and the most accurate and publicly available expectations. Based on the comparable motorway transactions analysed through the paper (A11, A7, R1), we assume that the investors would contemplate the following aspects in determining the final choice between the two alternative funding options. In Table 5.5, we have synthetized assumed characteristics of the potential term loan solution and the alternative project bond financing for the D4 motorway project. Our main focused variables will be the financing costs, leverage, maturity, drawdown and repayment profile, which will consequently have an impact on the other main characteristics of the financing structure.

These are the following.

a. Pricing – In the current market conditions, the "all-in" price (coupon, structuring fee, other transaction expenses) of a bond

DOI: 10.1057/9781137524041.0010

TABLE 5.5 *Scenario assumptions on bank loan and project bond for Slovakian D4 Motorway*

	Bank debt	Bond	
Amount	EUR 874 million	EUR 1,047 million	
Tenor	20 years	26 years	
Debt-to-Equity	77:23	90:10	
Ratios:			
ADSCR	1.25x	Net Debt/EBITDA	6.0x
LLCR	1.30x	FFO*/Debt	0.6x
		Cash Interest Coverage**	10.0x
		DSCR (FFO/DSA***)	2.0x
Distribution lock-up ratios:			
ADSCR	1.15x	n.a.	
LLCR	1.20x	n.a.	
Margin****		Coupon rate	
Construction	350bps p.a.	Fixed rate at 5.28%	
Operating	350bps p.a. until the 4th the anniversary of the actual completion date 375 bps p.a. until the 7th anniversary of the actual completion date 400 bps p.a. until the 9th anniversary of the actual completion date 425bps p.a. until the 15th anniversary of the actual completion date 450 bps p.a. from the 15th anniversary of the actual completion date		

DOI: 10.1057/9781137524041.0010

IRS rate	2.35% fixed rate	n.a.
Securities	• Asset pledge • Share pledge • Pledge on project documents • Pledge on rights under shareholder loans • Pledge on insurances • Direct agreements (grantor, D&C contractor; operator)	• Receivables, accounts and securities pledge • Subordinated debt receivables pledge • Issuer share pledge • Authority pledge
Arranging/ structuring fee	200bps	300bps
Commitment fee	140bps	n.a.
PBCE letter of credit	n.a.	EUR 200 million (Unfunded)
Bond rating	n.a.	[BBB+] (S&P)

Notes: * Funds from operations. It is calculated by adding depreciation and amortization expenses to earnings and deducting it for corporate taxes and VAT Payments

** (FFO-senior interest)/(Interest expense-non-cash interest)

*** Debt service annuity. Calculated as the payment for a bond amount on constant payments and a constant interest rate

**** Total interest rate= IRS rate + margin

Source: Authors' own research.

DOI: 10.1057/9781137524041.0010

financing often compares favourably to the term loan financing solution.

b. Drawdown profile can be much more customized (tailor-made) in the loan case. However, with the forward purchase agreements we can ensure deferred drawdown profile in bond financing as well (as have been the case in the Belgium A11 Motorway project).

c. Maturity/refinancing risk: Bonds for infrastructure assets are by nature long-term financing solutions. For PPPs, this can translate into financing solutions that can almost match PPP contract maturities and entail no refinancing risk. For the purpose of our demonstrating exercise, the maturity assumed is 26 years with a tail length, the amount of time between the maturity of the project debt and that of the project assumed life, of four years. A different story happens in case of commercial bank loan, where maturity can reach up to 20 years under the condition the amortization plan is fully respected. Therefore, the refinancing option is very likely to be undertaken by the project company, prolonging the tenor of the debt in the capital structure and hence benefit from leverage effects. However, a refinancing scenario will not be considered in our financial model as the aim is to show the main discrimination factors comparing the mentioned initial financing solutions.

d. Financial covenants and ratios: The bond solution is usually covenant lighter compared to a bank loan financing. In respect to cover ratios, for a bond financing, we need to consider different ratios than for a traditional PF loan. As we can observe in Table 5.5, in case of a project bond, we should calculate the following ratios to assess the financial riskiness of a project. However, the determination of minimum cover ratios is rather project specific, therefore the numbers are only approximations that serve our purpose and will be calculated based on our data from the financial model.

   - Net Debt/ EBITDA: It is a measure of a company's ability to pay off its incurred debt. This ratio gives the investor the approximate amount of time that would be needed to pay off all debt, ignoring the factors of interest, taxes, depreciation and amortization. It is a common metric used by credit rating agencies to assess the probability of defaulting on issued debt. A high level means that the firm may not be able to service its debt adequately. Conversely,

DOI: 10.1057/9781137524041.0010

a low ratio can suggest that the firm may opt to raise more debt if needed.

- FFO/Debt: A leverage ratio that a credit rating agency or an investor can use to evaluate a company's financial risk. The higher the FFO to debt ratio, the stronger the position the company in paying its debt from its operating income.
- Cash Interest Coverage: A ratio that informs about a company's ability to pay interest due to its creditors. However, it is calculated using accounting profits, which may not accurately reflect the actual amount of cash inflows available to the company to service its interest payments.
- DSCR (FFO/DSA): DSCR, in bond case, is calculated with different components compared to a bank loan DSCR; it especially includes the concession length by calculating a constant annuity debt service until the end of the project life.

e. Preparatory/structuring costs: Bond financing requires a bond rating which also determines the coupon rate. It brings some additional expenses to a borrower by preparing a prospectus on the bond issue for potential investors. Accordingly, the structuring costs are assumed to be higher in project bond solution.

f. Rating: The bonds are expected to be rated BBB+ (S&P), looking into Slovakian sovereign rating, project specific risk and involvement of EIB, which again improves the rating itself. In addition, we have taken a look into R1 project which also obtained BBB+, hence, we belief it is very reasonable.

g. We need to emphasize that apart from the financial structure itself, other project assumptions are identical (CAPEX, availability payments, construction period, other operating expenses and so on) and do not play an important role in the comparative analysis, therefore, we will not touch this topic more in details.

Overview of the testing results

Structuring the above-described assumptions into our financial model, we obtain the following results.

Firstly, we should look carefully at the sources and uses of funds for project bond and bank loan option in Tables 5.6 and 5.7, respectively, to spot the main differences. Debt amount is different comparing those two options due to the fact that the bank loan structure characteristics cannot sustain higher leverage. Since the debt amount is higher in the

DOI: 10.1057/9781137524041.0010

case of project bond, the total financing costs during the availability period exceed those of term loan. More interesting numbers to compare are in the right column of Tables 5.6 and 5.7. We see that the bank loan structure requires more than double the amount of shareholder funds (equity and shareholder loans) to fund the project cost with the debt size being maximized. A higher proportion of equity contribution goes hand in hand with a lower percentage of debt raised, what is definitely not in the interest of sponsor. In base case scenario, the PBCE facility is not and neither should be drawn (PBCE = 0), since it steps in only in case of unexpected construction cost overruns (unfunded PBCE). Clearly, in the bank loan case, the PBCE tool is not involved.

Finally, we have obtained the following results looking at the very important KPIs for the sponsor when comparing the financing solutions undertaken which are illustrated in Table 5.8. The equity contribution is much lower in the bond case, and we can see that NPV and IRR of the shareholders are higher, demonstrating a better return on the

TABLE 5.6 *D4 Project estimated source and uses of funds – project bond case*

Uses of funds	in million EUR	%	Source of funds	in million EUR	%
CAPEX	900.5	74%	Shareholder funds	114.0	9%
Financing costs	190.0	16%			
Project costs	52.5	4%	Project bond	1047.3	86%
MRA funding	1.3	0%	PBCE	0	0%
DSRA funding	12.3	1%	Income (operations)	60.4	5%
SPV costs	65.1	5%			
Total	1221.7	100%	Total	1221.7	100%

TABLE 5.7 *D4 Project estimated source and uses of funds – bank loan case*

Uses of funds	in million EUR	%	Source of funds	in million EUR	%
CAPEX	900.5	75%	Shareholder funds	261.0	22%
Financing costs	166.3	14%			
Project costs	50.0	4%	Term loan	874.0	73%
MRA funding	1.3	0%			
DSRA funding	12.3	1%	Income (operations)	60.5	5%
SPV costs	65.1	5%			
Total	1195.5	100%	Total	1195.5	100%

DOI: 10.1057/9781137524041.0010

TABLE 5.8 *D4 Project estimated NPV and IRR – project bond versus bank loan*

NPV and IRR	Project Bond	Bank Loan
Equity NPV	EUR 57 million	EUR 46 million
IRR equity	13.94%	11.43%
IRR debt	5.82%	7.33%

Source: Authors' own research based on scenario assumptions.

shareholders' capital employed in comparison to the bank loan structure. Apart from that, the total cost of debt is higher in the term loan case with 7.33 per cent compared to 5.8 per cent in the bond case. Thus, we can conclude from Table 5.8 evidence that the project bond should be the preferred financing option to be undertaken from the shareholders' side. Moreover, looking at the payback period is again in favour of project bonds, enabling much quicker repayment of shareholders' invested money (9.92 years versus 14.93 years).

As mentioned above, the bond financial structure requires different financial cover ratios than traditional PF loan transactions. They act as the main indicators for the assessment of project's financial risk. Taking into account the financial structure, we have calculated the main ratios to show the financial risk of the selected project, which can be seen in Table 5.9. According to Moody's rating scale, the project bond under our assumptions would receive a rating of Baa1.

Regarding the planned senior debt outstanding during the project life, we can model the profile in the bond case in a similar way to the loan term case, albeit with a longer maturity. Thus, we can have an amortized loan alike picture. This was obtained by adopting the project bond innovative Belgium A11 Motorway drawdown (forward purchase agreements) and amortized repayment profile (different bond maturities). Looking at the A11 structure, we slightly decreased the tenor, being more consistent in comparison with term loan and still are able to show advantageous financial structure involving project bond with PBCE support.

Discrimination factors: Bank loan versus project bond

Finally, we recap the main discrimination factors of our comparative analysis.

a. **Different financing cost**

   All-in financing costs mainly depend on the interest/coupon rate and on the fees payable for structuring the financing of the

DOI: 10.1057/9781137524041.0010

TABLE 5.9 *Bond financing estimated cover ratios in D4 project*

Ratios	Average	Max.*	Min.*
Cash Interest Coverage	9.84	42.44	4.35
FFO/Debt	0.64	5.01	0.16
DSCR (FFO/DSA)	2.24	4.76	1.89
Net debt/EBITDA	5.48	9.32	0.32

Notes: * Maximum and minimum value of the ratio during the lifetime of the project
Source: Authors' own research based on scenario assumptions.

transaction, commitment fees and so on. Project bond financing costs are usually determined in a book-building process where the credit rating of the project, the liquidity on the capital markets and the perceived riskiness of the transaction by bond investors play an important role. The benchmarking exercise considering the R1 Motorway bond issue in late 2013 and A11 bond issue in 2014 is fundamental for the assumed credit rating. Two differences were spotted comparing the projects. On the one hand, there was no construction risk for investors in R1 compared to D4; and on the other hand, in D4, there is involvement of EIB's PBCE, which basically mitigates the construction risk and ensures a similar or the same investment-rating grade. Our assumption is that those two effects cancel out each other, and the overall effect on the credit rating should be neglected. Therefore, the coupon rate assumed for the D4 transaction is 5.28 per cent on annual basis.

Bank loan interest rate assumption is related to R1 Motorway financing as well and takes into account the analyzed banking landscape and current market conditions. In the assumptions described in Table 5.5, we assumed a step up margin starting with 350 bps in construction period and stepping up to the level of 450 bps through the tenor period (IRS at 2.35 per cent level).

In current market conditions, the total financing cost of bond facility often compares favourably to the term loan financing solution. We can observe the same in our assumptions, with another big difference in tenor (maturity period), which has a big impact on the maximum debt capacity and the leverage that can be supported by the project for the different financing options.

In addition, in the project bond case, shareholders' dividends are paid on a regular basis throughout the concession period and much earlier than in the case of the term loan where loan specific financial covenants do not allow dividend payouts in the first years.

b. **Leverage throughout concession**

With leveraging the equity, we increase the potential return of an investment for a shareholder in case the project IRR is higher than the cost of debt. Leverage helps both the investor and the firm to invest or operate, but it brings along greater risk. In the business world, a company can use leverage to try to generate shareholder wealth, but if it fails to do so, the interest expense and credit risk of default destroys shareholder value by the potential restructuring of the company in case defaulting loans are accelerated by the creditors. To sum up, a high leverage magnifies both gains and losses.

The repayment profile plays an important role when defining the leverage throughout the project life. In case of an amortized term loan, we are basically deleveraging the transaction gradually. Meanwhile, with bond financing, we assume a back loaded repayment profile, sometimes as a bullet at the final repayment date, maintaining a higher level of debt through the project for a longer period.

Looking at the leverage level at the beginning of the transaction, in a bank loan scenario, due to the shorter maturity and minimum repayments, the structure cannot sustain a higher than 77:23 debt-to-equity ratio. In the case of a project bond, we can have a different picture with leverage up to 90 per cent, mainly due to the fact of longer maturity.

In addition, leverage is decisive in determining the company's tax shield level. Typically, higher leverage also means higher financing costs, which decrease the tax base for income tax payments and brings additional added value to the shareholders.

c. **Equity**

As we have already mentioned above, the equity contribution is considerably higher in case of term loan financing to successfully support the transaction features. The equity invested in the bond case amount to EUR 114 m while in term loan solution is more than twice as big and reaches EUR 261 m. If we tend to increase the leverage in the term loan scenario, the debt servicing with such maturity is not supported. In addition, we need to take into account the requirements to meet minimum ADSCR.

DOI: 10.1057/9781137524041.0010

At this point, we can raise a question about the availability of equity for such a transaction with considerable financing requirements. Are there really enough funds available from the project sponsors and their co-investors to fulfil this gap? This question makes term loan financing structure very questionable in our case.

d. Tax shield

One of the main benefits of having debt financing is the tax-deductibility of interest payments. A reduction in taxable income for a corporation is achieved through claiming allowable deductions such as debt interest, amortization and depreciation. These deductions reduce the taxpayers' taxable income for a given year or defer income taxes into future years. Tax-efficient investing strategies are a cornerstone of investing for high-net-worth individuals and corporations, whose annual tax bills can be very high.

As described before, in the case of deleveraging the transaction or gradually repaying the debt principal, financing costs are reduced through the period and the base amount, from which income taxes are extracted, is increasing (fully amortized term loan structure). On the other side, in the case of bond financing, the debt amount remains higher throughout the concession period, and it is repaid with back loaded instalments. This characteristic guarantees a higher tax shield (along with higher financing cost) and consequently savings in corporate taxes.

However, while having a larger corporate tax shield, we also recognize the higher possibility of having trapped cash in the project company.

e. Trapped cash

Trapped cash refers to the portion of a company's cash that is held on a company's cash balance, normally in a proceeds or current account. The cash payout to shareholders is restricted by net profits and retained earnings from accounting, in a sense that retained earnings are not high enough as the generated cash from operations. In a typical tax and accounting legislation, these funds cannot be distributed to shareholders who have to wait for upcoming net profits to be generated. This is one reason for available cash to be withheld or "trapped" in the project company.

Dividend restriction covenants protect debt holders by reducing the cash payout to shareholders in case certain performance

DOI: 10.1057/9781137524041.0010

ratios cannot be met. Thus, from the perspective of shareholders, restrictions on dividend payment are more likely to reduce shareholder value. This trapped cash can be paid out only in case of a refinancing or at the end of maturity, when financial covenants are cancelled. The big disadvantage of trapped cash is that the return on the trapped cash is minimal (deposit interest rate or other safe financial asset return around or less than 1–2 per cent) while shareholders require much higher rate of returns for their invested funds (minimum 10–12 per cent).

At this point, we can raise the question of time value of the money, since we are aware that money available at the present time is worth more than the same amount in the future due to its potential earning capacity (additional interest). We must mention that in our case, we have not considered the quantitative effect in respect to the trapped cash.

5.2.5 Reasons why Project bond should be the best solution for D4 Motorway

Throughout our discussion, we have analyzed a few real world cases from which we can extract the most important characteristics and financial structures and used them as a benchmark for the new Slovakian D4 Motorway deal. Relying on the information we have assessed, we can clearly confirm that the project bond financing option with EIB's PBCE instrument involved can be one of the very suitable and few available financing option for the project due to the following facts.

- Since the Slovakian sovereign credit risk, in January 2015, is rated A/A+/A2 (S&P, Fitch, Moody's), it is realistic that the project bond for a well-structured viable infrastructure PPP transaction could easily reach a BBB- grade. We need to emphasize that eventually the PBCE would trigger the bond rating one to two notches higher, which is fundamental to bond pricing and locating an investors' appetite for such an instrument. This would certainly attract a wide range of institutional and other investors across the European investment grade space. In addition, pension funds, insurance companies and other institutional investors are seeking to diversify their current investment portfolio and invest in assets with yields higher than government bonds delivering stable, long-term income, which would match their liabilities perfectly.

DOI: 10.1057/9781137524041.0010

- EIB could potentially act as anchor investor and purchase a certain number of bonds for its portfolio, triggering the good investment picture for the project and further attracting interest from investors.
- PPP infrastructure project based on availability fee payments: No demand risk component (traffic and market risk) and in respect to the construction risk, the EIB involvement, with an available letter of credit, acts as a big risk mitigant in case of cash shortfalls during construction period.
- Good track record of recent project bonds issuances in Europe such as the successful issue of project bonds for refinancing of R1 Motorway in Slovakia and greenfield infrastructure PPP finance of A11 Motorway in Belgium with EIB involvement.
- Conventional bank lending long-term tenor availability is becoming a disturbing fact for project sponsors due to the imposed regulations from Basel III and additional liquidity buffer costs added on top of funding costs, making overall pricing more expensive. However, we consider that this option very likely includes a refinance risk, which project sponsors often try to shift to the public side aiming at cheaper, albeit shorter, bank lending and better value for money concept. Again, this is difficult strategy to conduct and not possible every time. Therefore, project bond solution is a reasonable alternative solution, which with its long maturity does not involve any refinancing risk.
- In respect to the pricing, in such a large CAPEX deal along with prospective dynamics of banking lending, we can expect a pricing advantage for the financing structure with project bonds, with involvement of mentioned PBCE, and will certainly bring more value for money in the future compared to a bank loan.
- The recently closed transaction, Belgium A11 Motorway, possesses very innovative financial features. Issues such as negative carry, drawdown profile and cost overrun mechanism were carefully addressed and very successfully resolved. Therefore, the D4 transaction should implement those best practices to deal with these issues.

DOI: 10.1057/9781137524041.0010

Conclusion

Abstracts: *We have provided an insight into the European market comparing project bond funding to conventional bank lending as an alternative financing solution for infrastructure project finance. We have seen the real benefits from the EIB Project Bond Initiative, how it is applied to the real examples and its main requirements to become applicable.*

Our analysis helps to understand the conditions which need to be met to enable a project bond as a suitable financing solution. On top of that, we are able to identify the main innovative features of project bonds in combination with the Project Bond Credit Enhancement scheme.

Rossi, Emanuele and Rok Stepic. *Infrastructure Project Finance and Project Bonds in Europe.* Basingstoke: Palgrave Macmillan, 2015.
DOI: 10.1057/9781137524041.0011.

The real world case studies have showed that in the near future project bonds, as alternative financing (with adequate construction support instrument) in certain greenfield infrastructure projects, can play an important role. While comparing the traditional bank loan to project bond we have noticed several discrimination factors, which determine the beneficial financing structure. We realize that projects with significant total project costs (above EUR 400 million) require longer tenors or much lower leverage to match the required debt service and need to provide shareholders with certain returns from the very beginning of the operational period of an asset, which can be normally obtained only by a bond issue. Taking into consideration the negative developments in the banking sector (additional regulations), we can assume that institutional investors will have an important role in PF, with their large pools of available funds.

Clearly, the project by itself needs to have certain characteristics in order to be suitable for bond funding (PPP, project country, bankability of project structure, certain insurance of revenues as in normal PPP scheme, strong and reliable sponsors). Based on this, we can conclude that project bonds will most likely be present only in financing arrangements in infrastructural sectors which enjoy the support of governmental authorities and organizations.

From the underlying case studies analysis, we could learn that projects, which implement a project bond funding structure, show a promising rate of success. It can be seen that additional synergies can be created, as well as additional value can be generated for the benefit of shareholders. Furthermore, we could observe that the pool of investors involved in A11 and R1 motorway deals and others mentioned infrastructural transactions was significant and very diversified, which confirms a great interest from the European capital/debt market for the infrastructure project bonds asset class.

Moreover, the Slovakian D4 prospective transaction described in Chapter 5 would represent an important milestone for the whole CEE region, since this transaction would be the first of this kind where a PPP project would be financed with a project bond. We decided to leave enough space to discuss it as it would represent the first greenfield project in the CEE supported by PBCE or similar instruments, creating a fundamental template for many other prospective deals in the region. It will be a great challenge for all parties involved in the transaction, such as politicians and practitioners, to find an alternative financing for the D4 Motorway project.

DOI: 10.1057/9781137524041.0011

Besides that, we have emphasized only EIB PBI credit enhancement solution even though there are several other supportive instruments on the market (for example PEBBLE), which have a different impact on a project financial structure. Therefore, the parties involved should consider other aspects as well, which could end up playing a decisive role in raising funding in the future. In addition, our research was mainly focused on Europe regions; hence, further research could be performed by including other markets/regions while analyzing project funding options, since the needs for infrastructure are significant in emerging markets and other less developed countries where project bonds as a financing solution are not very likely to be undergone.

In order to conclude, our analysis presented an alternative financing solution to the typically sourced traditional banking loan, which is/will be, in our opinion, strongly impacted and constrained by new banking regulations and will not be a suitable funding solution in regards to providing enough funds to meet all upcoming infrastructure project financing in the near future. Moreover, compared to a couple of years ago, a project bond market in Europe is now active and growing. Institutional investment has become a key feature of the market and this is expected to continue and strengthen. The PBI has had a strong catalytic effect in promoting capital market financing and in widening access to institutional funding. A wider use of PBCE is anticipated in the future to support public investment needs via financial instruments. In this context, the new EU Investment Plan for Europe, with its aims to mobilizing private investment through the multiplier effect of the newly created European Fund for Strategic Investments (EFSI), represents the last move in attracting private investors to stimulate investment in the infrastructure sector and responding to market gaps, in which the debt/bond capital market can have a huge role to play in the future. Meanwhile, we clearly have to wait and see in which way EFSI, once fully established, will operate.

However, with a certain project bond track record, investors' comfort will increase to such a point that project bonds will be considered as a very useful instrument for funding infrastructure projects.

DOI: 10.1057/9781137524041.0011

Appendices

A.1 *Risks and their mitigants in a motorway project example*

Risk type	Issue	Mitigants
Construction Period		
Design risk	Responsibility for the design of the works	Passed down to the constructor under the D&C contract
General construction risk	Risks related to the design, construction, completion and defect rectification	Born by the constructor; protection through adequate security package and supported by parent company guarantee
Cost overruns	Risk of rising construction costs	Fully assumed by the D&C contractor under the fixed lump sum price contract
Construction delays	Risks related to the timely completion of all project works within the set target dates	Fully passed down to the constructor; cash protection by way of robust LD regime
Permits and land acquisition	Risk of obtaining all relevant zoning and building permits	Risks of existing permits lays with the Public Authority; only minor remaining permits stay with the D&C contractor
Ground conditions	Risk of unforeseen or unexpected ground conditions	Passed down to the D&C contractor
Macroeconomics risks		
Interest rate	Increase of interest rates	Project co. will enter into interest rate hedging arrangement for 95% of the senior term Loan
Inflation risk	Raising cost due to inflation	Passed down to the D&C contractor

DOI: 10.1057/9781137524041.0012

Operation Period		
Macroeconomic risk		
Interest rate	Increase of interest rates	Interest rate hedging arrangements during the Operation period for 100% of the senior term loan Facility
Inflation risk	Raising cost due to inflation	Partially offset by indexation of adjustment of that part of the availability payments that are expected to cover exposed variable costs
Cost overruns		
Operation and routine maintenance	Risk of increasing operating costs	Fixed price O&M contract for the entire concession period, subject to inflation adjustment
		Greenfield construction works reduce the risk of latent defects
Heavy maintenance	Projection of future heavy maintenance costs	Shareholder's extensive experience in planning of lifecycle costs
		Active market allows competitive tendering of works.
Handback	Project co. will need to carry out any necessary renewal works to meet handback requirements at its cost	The scheduled routine and the heavy maintenance works shall ensure an appropriate condition of the road. Any additional handback works will occur when senior debt will be repaid
Market risks		
Traffic risk	Traffic exposure	No traffic risk: remuneration is availability-based, thus no toll revenue risk
Performance risks		
Lower unitary charge	The payment mechanism is subject to deductions for unavailability, performance and safety	No particular difficult road for operation. The mandated operator is a very experienced road operator
Change in law	Law risk exposure	Discriminatory and specific change in law is fully assumed by the public authority

DOI: 10.1057/9781137524041.0012

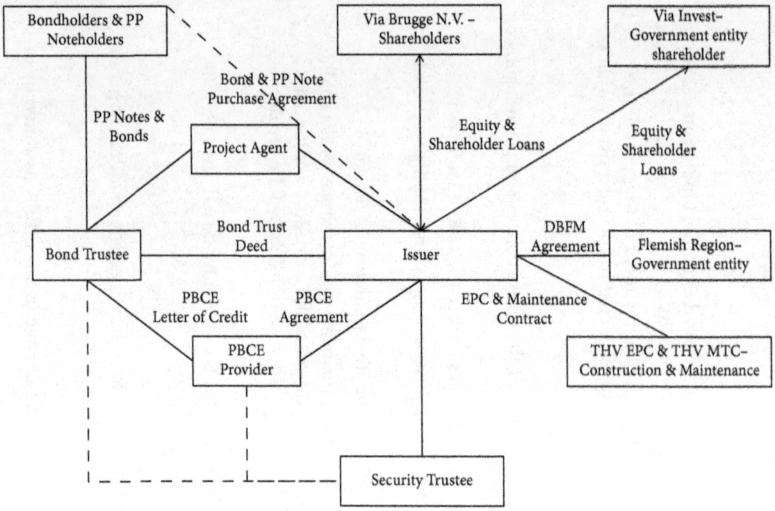

A.2 *Transaction structure of Belgium A11 Motorway*

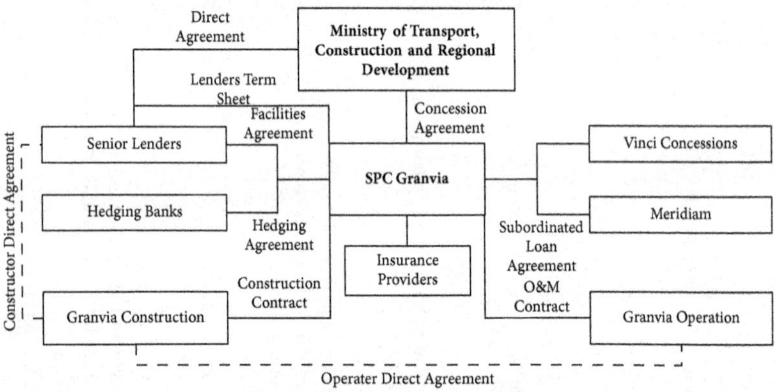

A.3 *Project contractual structure of Slovakia R1 Motorway*

DOI: 10.1057/9781137524041.0012

Bibliography

Basel Committee on Banking Supervision (2006). *International Convergence of Capital Measurement and Capital Standards. A Revised Framework,* at http://bis.org/publ/bcbs128.htm, date accessed 5 December 2014.

R. Bird, H. Liem and S. Thorp (2012). "'Infrastructure: Real Assets and Real Returns'", *European Financial Management,* n. 4, 802–24.

F. Bitsch, A. Buchner and C. Kaserer (2010). "Risk, Return and Cash Flow Characteristics of Infrastructure Fund Investments", *EIB Papers,* 15, 106–136.

F. Blanc-Brude (2014). *Benchmarking Long-Term Investment in Infrastructure. Objectives, Roadmap and Recent Progress* (EDHEC--Risk Institute).

C. Bradley, J. McLaren and S. Corlett (2012). *Is the Bond Market the Way Forward for Project Finance?* (Hong Kong: Linklaters).

E. Chan and M. Worth (2011). "'Basel III and Project Finance'", *Project Finance International Issue,* 460, 15–22.

Deloitte (2014). *Project Bonds: An Alternative Source of Financing Infrastructure Projects,* http://www2.deloitte.com (home page), date accessed 16 January 2015.

EIB (2010). *Capital Markets in PPP Financing: Where We Were and Where Are We Going?,* http://www.eib.org/epec/ (home page), date accessed 15 September 2014.

EIB (2012a) *An Outline Guide to Project Bonds Credit Enhancement and the Project Bond Initiative,* http://www.eib.org (home page), date accessed 15 September 2014.

DOI: 10.1057/9781137524041.0013

EIB (2012b). *Financing PPPs with Project Bonds,* http://www.eib.org/epec/ (home page), date accessed 15 September 2014.

EIB (2013). *Interim Report on the Pilot Phase of the Europe 2020 Project Bond Initiative,* http://www.eib.org (home page), date accessed 5 December 2014.

S. Gatti (2013). *Project Finance in Theory and Practice,* 2nd edn (London: Elsevier inc).

Deutsche Bank (2013) *Project Bond Initiative,* https://www.dbresearch.com/ (home page), date accessed 18 January 2015.

Deutsche Bank, Asset & Wealth Management (2014). *European Infrastructure Update 2014,* https://institutional.deutscheawm.com (home page), date accessed 16 December 2014.

ING (2014). *Insight Central & Eastern Europe,* https://www.ing.nl (home page), date accessed 17 September 2014.

InfraNews (2014). *Project Bond Reinvented,* www.infra-news.com (home page), date accessed 18 September 2014.

Moody's (2009). *Default and Recovery Rates for Project Finance Debts, 1992--2008,* http://www.moodys.com (home page), date accessed 1 December 2014.

Moody's (2010). *Default and Recovery Rates for Project Finance Bank Loans, 1983--2008,* http://www.moodys.com (home page), date accessed 10 December 2014.

Moody's (2015). *Default and Recovery Rates for Project Finance Bank Loans, 1983--2013,* http://www.moodys.com (home page), date accessed 10 March 2015.

OECD (2013). *The Potential of Private Institutional Investors for Financing Transport Infrastructure,* Discussion Paper n.14 http://www.internationaltransportforum.org (home page), date accessed 5 December 2014.

Oxford Economics (2013). *Sizing the Global Infrastructure Market,* http://www.oxfordeconomics.com (home page), date accessed 17 December 2014.

Preqin Infrastructure Online (2014). *The 2014 Preqin Global Infrastructure Report,* https://www.preqin.com (home page), date accessed 02 February 2015.

PWC (2013a). *Capital Markets: The Rise of Non-Bank Infrastructure Project Finance* http://www.pwc.com (home page), date accessed 16 November 2014.

DOI: 10.1057/9781137524041.0013

PWC (2013b). *Capital Project and Infrastructure Spending*, http://www.pwc.com (home page), date accessed 15 August 2014.

R. J. Sawant (2010). *Infrastructure Investing: Managing Risks and Rewards for Pensions, Insurance Companies and Endowments* (Hoboken, NJ USA: Wiley & Sons Publishers).

B. Weber and H. W. Alfen (2010). *Infrastructure as an Asset Class: Investment Strategies, Project Finance and PPP* (London: Wiley & Sons Publishers).

E. R. Yescombe (2013). *Principles of Project Finance* (Oxford: Elsevier).

DOI: 10.1057/9781137524041.0013

Index

DOI: 10.1057/9781137524041.0014

DOI: 10.1057/9781137524041.0014

DOI: 10.1057/9781137524041.0014

DOI: 10.1057/9781137524041.0014

DOI: 10.1057/9781137524041.0014

CPSIA information can be obtained at www.ICGtesting.com
Printed in the USA
BVOW08*2337030816

457806BV00012BA/98/P